SCHOLASTIC

Cut & Paste Mini-Books

Science

NANCY I. SANDERS

New York • Toronto • London • Auckland • Sydney
Mexico City • New Delhi • Hong Kong • Buenos Aires

D0814356

Teaching
Resources

To Mr. Paul Shotts, from Everett Area High School, who was my eighth grade science teacher. The thrill of mixing chemicals, observing amazing reactions, and exploring basic scientific principles in your classroom ignited a love for science that still burns bright today. Thanks for your years of dedication and inspiration to the many students from my hometown.

To Mr. Arthur Smith, from Everett Area High School, whose memory still lives on in the hearts of many, and who taught me, along with others, to love Chemistry and Physics.

Edited by Immacula A. Rhodes
Cover design by Wendy Chan
Interior illustrations by Lucia Kemp Henry
Interior design by Holly Grundon

ISBN: 978-0-439-57408-2

Contents

Mini-Book	Skill	Page

Introduction

Welcome *to Cut & Paste Mini-Books: Science*! These 15 mini-books raise the use of manipulatives to a fun and educational level. Designed to enhance your curriculum, the stories reinforce important standards-based science concepts and literacy skills as children read the text and glue patterns onto the corresponding pages to demonstrate comprehension.

In the mini-books, you'll find a collection of science-driven stories that include high-frequency words and controlled vocabulary. The text is just right for helping beginning readers build word recognition, fluency, and other literacy skills. Built-in science concepts align with the Mid-continent Research for Education and Learning (McREL) standards for Kindergarten and first grade, giving children the opportunity to work with key science topics such as plant growth, animal homes, the five senses, nutrition, seasons, weather, and space. Each story prompts children to think about a specific science concept and then respond by gluing patterns onto the pages to complete the book.

Everything you need to make the mini-books is here. As children follow the directions to assemble the books, they'll get additional practice in sequencing and building fine motor skills. Each reproducible mini-book includes patterns that children cut out and paste onto the pages. Suggestions for introducing the featured science concepts are provided to help you prepare children to complete the book successfully. The extension activities let you take the concept a step further to help reinforce it.

Children will love revisiting these stories again and again. As they read, they'll enjoy reviewing key science concepts in a fun, unique way. In addition, children will gain confidence in word recognition and reading fluency with repeated readings. But don't keep all the fun at school—encourage children to take the mini-books home, where they can continue and share their learning excitement with their families!

Using the Mini-Books

Once children have assembled their mini-books and cut out the patterns, you might walk them through the pages as a preview before they glue the pieces in place. Here are some suggestions for doing this:

❋ Ask children to place all of the patterns face up near their mini-book.

❋ Beginning with the cover, read aloud the text on each page.

❋ As you preview each right-hand page, encourage children to use clues from the text on the spread to decide which pattern belongs on the page. Invite them to place the pattern on the page (but not glue it in place at this time), and then read the text again. Does the pattern make sense with the text? When finished, ask them to put the pattern back with the others.

✽ When you preview page 11 of the mini-book (the last page), talk about what children need to do to complete the activity. If desired, work together to find the answers, but have children wait until later to fill in the answers.

✽ After previewing the mini-book together, have children read it by themselves. This time, ask them to glue each pattern to its corresponding page and complete the activity on page 11.

Assembling the Mini-Books

The cut-and-paste mini-books require very few materials, and children can complete them at their desk or at a learning center. To get started, provide children with copies of the reproducible pages for the selected mini-book, then demonstrate the steps below. (Or you might assemble the books in advance.)

Materials
✽ scissors

✽ crayons or markers

✽ glue stick or paste

✽ stapler

1. Fold the front cover/page 1 in half along the solid center line. Keep the fold to the right side.

2. Repeat step 1 for each of the remaining page pairs: pages 2/3, 4/5, 6/7, 8/9, and 10/11. Stack the pages in order with the cover on top and all of the folds on the right side.

3. Staple the pages together along the left edge.

Connections to the Standards

Mid-continent Research for Education and Learning (McREL), a nationally recognized nonprofit organization, has compiled and evaluated national and state standards—and proposed what teachers should provide for their K–1 students to grow proficient in science and reading. The activities in this book support the following standards:

Science

Life Science

* Knows that plants and animals closely resemble their parents
* Knows that living things go through a process of growth and change
* Knows the basic needs of plants and animals
* Knows that plants and animals have features that help them live in different environments
* Understands that living things have similar needs
* Knows that plants and animals need certain resources for energy and growth

Earth and Space Sciences

* Knows vocabulary for different kinds of weather (e.g., rainy, windy, sunny)
* Knows how the environment changes over the seasons
* Knows that weather conditions can change daily
* Knows vocabulary (clouds, Sun, moon) used to describe major features of the sky
* Knows basic patterns of the Sun and moon
* Knows that stars are innumerable, unevenly dispersed, and of unequal brightness

Behavioral Studies

Understands that interactions among learning, inheritance, and physical development affect human behavior

* Knows that people use their senses to find out about their surroundings and themselves and that different senses provide different information

Health

* Knows that some foods are more nutritious than others
* Classifies foods according to food groups
* Knows basic personal hygiene habits required to maintain health

Reading

Uses the general skills and strategies of the reading process including:

* Uses mental images and meaning clues based on pictures and print to aid in comprehension of text
* Uses basic elements of phonetic and structural analysis to decode unknown words
* Understands level-appropriate sight words and vocabulary
* Uses self-correction strategies

Kendall, J. S., & Marzano, R. J. (2004). *Content knowledge: A compendium of standards and benchmarks for K–12 education*. Aurora, CO: Mid-continent Research for Education and Learning. Online database: http://www.mcrel.org/standards-benchmarks/

Matt's Pictures

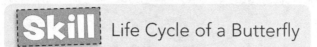

Skill Life Cycle of a Butterfly

Getting Started

Work with children to list facts they already know about butterflies. Write each fact on a separate construction-paper butterfly cutout. Display the facts on a bulletin board. Then, to enrich children's butterfly knowledge, share new facts with them, such as "butterflies are insects," "butterflies live all over the world," "butterflies are symmetrical," "butterflies have two pairs of wings," and "butterflies drink nectar from flowers." Write each new fact on a butterfly cutout and add it to the display.

Completing the Mini-Book

Ask children to write their name on the cover, then cut out and glue the patterns onto the pages, as shown. Finally, have them complete the activity on the last page.

Reproducible Pages
mini-book: pages 8–13
patterns: page 14

Matt's Pictures

by _____

① One day Matt saw a tiny egg on a leaf. He took a picture. Click!

②

③ Soon Matt saw a very small caterpillar. He took a picture. Click!

④

⑤ When Matt looked again, he saw a big, fat caterpillar. He took a picture. Click!

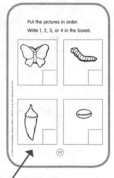

⑥ Then Matt saw a chrysalis hanging from a leaf. He took a picture. Click!

⑦

⑧

⑨ At last, Matt saw a beautiful butterfly. He took a picture. Click! Then he took his pictures to school for Show and Tell.

⑩

⑪ Put the pictures in order. Write 1, 2, 3, or 4 in the boxes.

Put the pictures in order.

Taking It Further

Ask children to color, cut out, and glue a copy of each of the five patterns (page 14) to a separate index card. Have them glue the cards to craft sticks to make puppets. Then form small groups and instruct children to make up skits about butterflies using their stick puppets. If desired, drape a length of colorful fabric over a table to make a simple puppet stage. Invite groups to use the stage when they perform their skits for the class.

One day Matt saw

a tiny egg on a leaf.

He took a picture.

Click!

Matt's Pictures

by _____

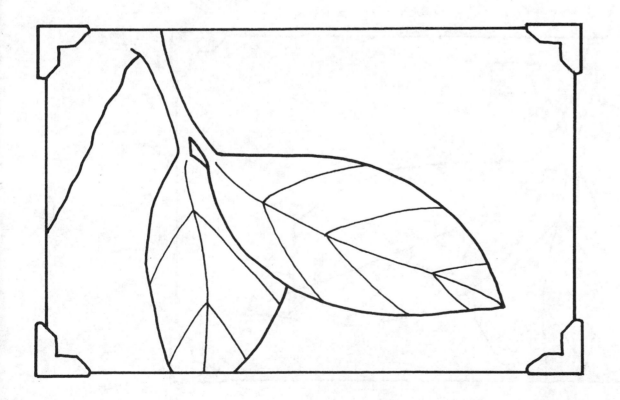

Soon Matt saw
a very small caterpillar.

He took a picture.

Click!

③

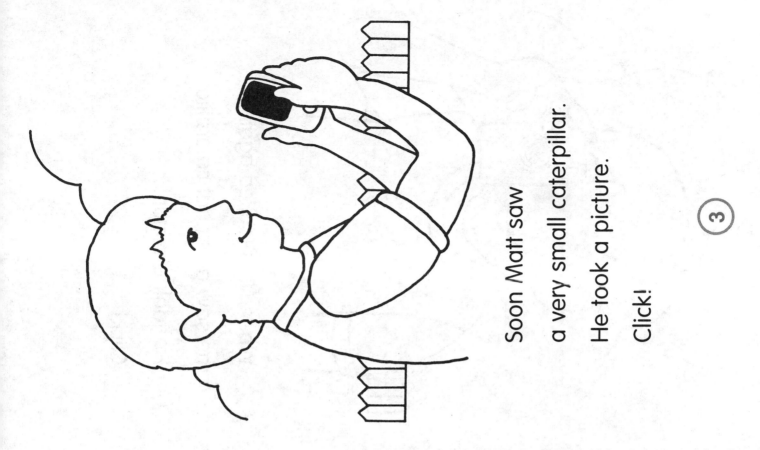

②

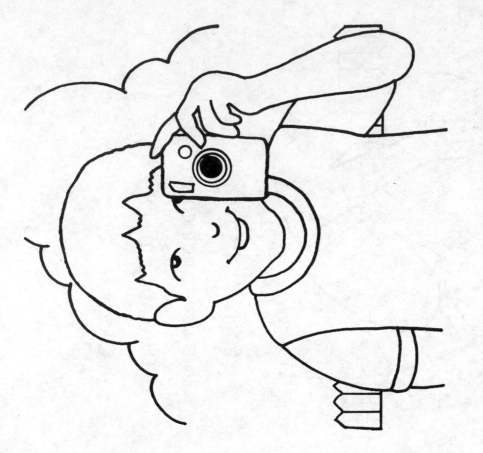

When Matt looked again,

he saw a big, fat caterpillar.

He took a picture.

Click!

⑤

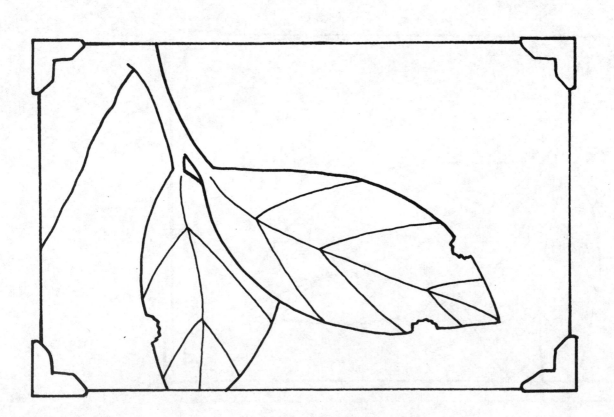

④

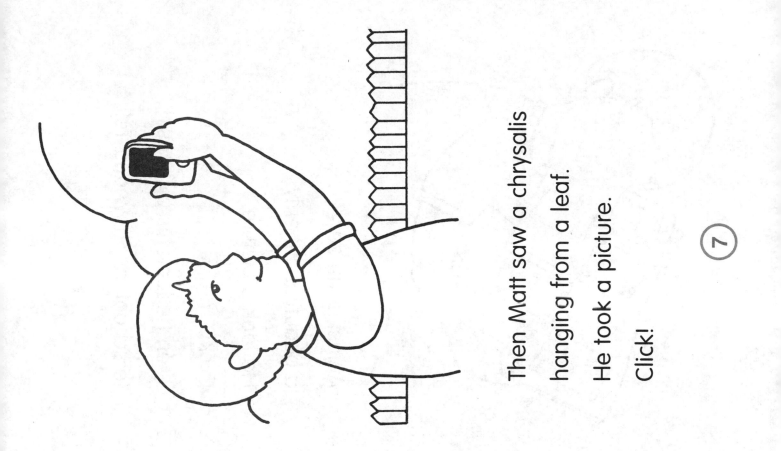

Then Matt saw a chrysalis
hanging from a leaf.

He took a picture.

Click!

(7)

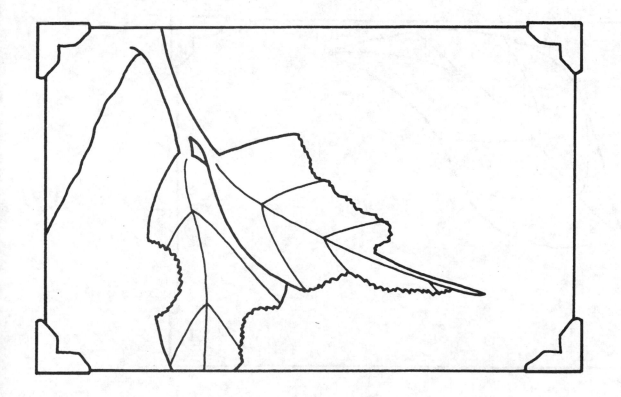

(6)

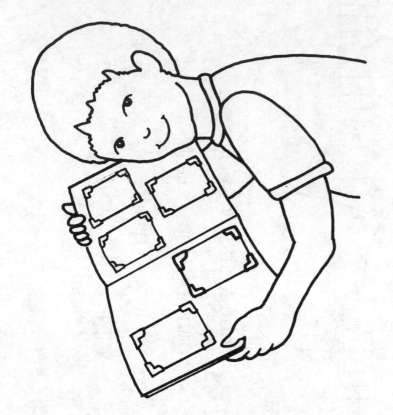

At last, Matt saw
a beautiful butterfly.

He took a picture.

Click!

Then he took his pictures

to school for Show and Tell.

⑨

Cut & Paste Mini-Books: Science © 2011 by Nancy I. Sanders, Scholastic Teaching Resources (page 12)

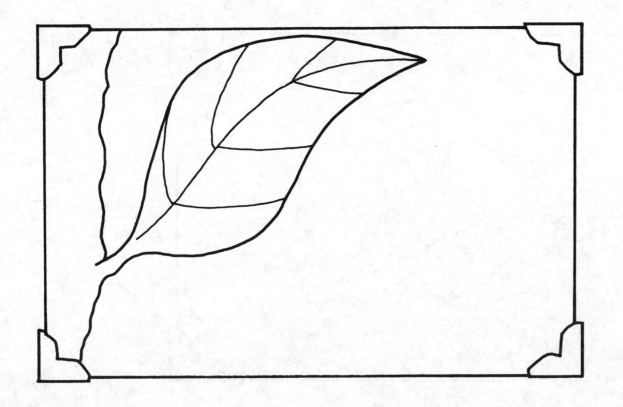

⑧

Put the pictures in order.
Write 1, 2, 3, or 4 in the boxes.

Cut & Paste Mini-Books: Science © 2011 by Nancy I. Sanders, Scholastic Teaching Resources (page 13)

11

10

Matt's Pictures
Cut & Paste Patterns

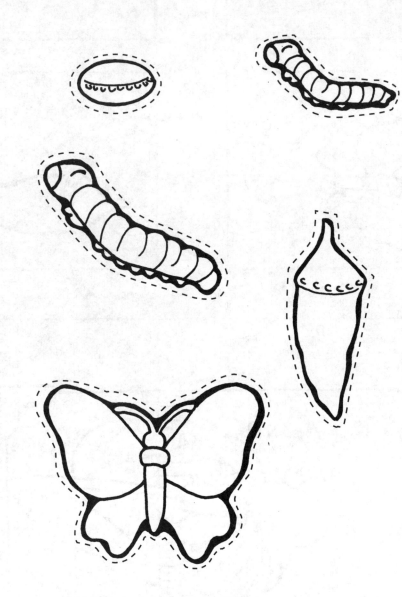

Busy Bees

Getting Started

To demonstrate how pollination works, put two large construction-paper flowers at opposite ends of the room. Place a small paper plate in the center of each flower. Sprinkle white flour on one plate and cinnamon powder on the other. Then distribute cotton balls to one small group at a time. Have children pretend they are bees flying from one flower to the other. As they go, have them dip their cotton ball in each flower's center. Point out how the flour and cinnamon mix with each other—much like what happens when real bees carry pollen from flower to flower.

Completing the Mini-Book

Ask children to write their name on the cover, then cut out and glue the patterns onto the pages, as shown. Finally, have them complete the activity on the last page.

Reproducible Pages
mini-book:
pages 16–21
patterns: page 22

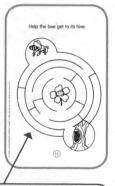

Help the bee to get its hive.

Taking It Further

Discuss different jobs that bees do in a beehive, such as making the honeycomb, feeding the young, cleaning the hive, and guarding the entrance. Then talk about jobs children can do in the classroom. Afterward, set up a rotation system to assign class jobs to children. Also, have small groups make posters about jobs children can do at any time, such as picking up trash, cleaning a center before leaving it, and putting away supplies after use.

15

Look over there.

Do you see that bee?

He's helping build a hive

in that big old tree.

Busy Bees

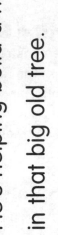

by _____

Watch that bee dance
for other bees he meets.
He tells them where to go
to get nectar, so sweet.

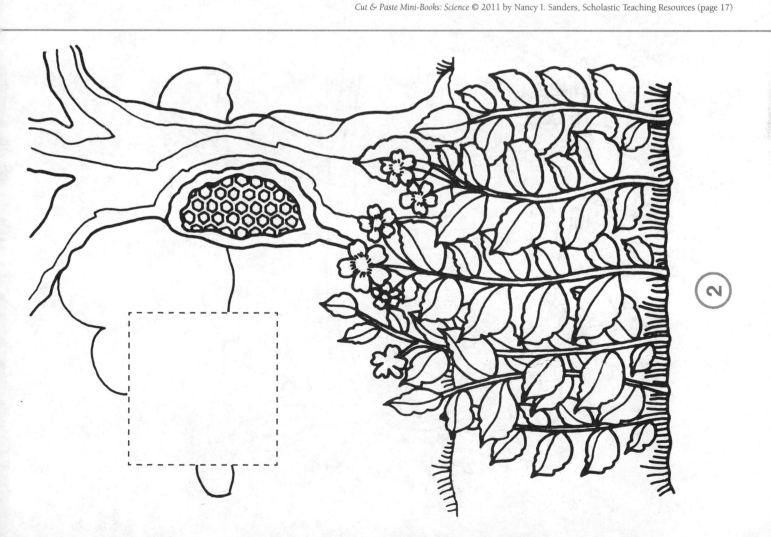

2

The bees fly to the flowers
and drink from the blooms.

When they finish there,
off again they zoom.

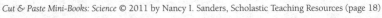

5

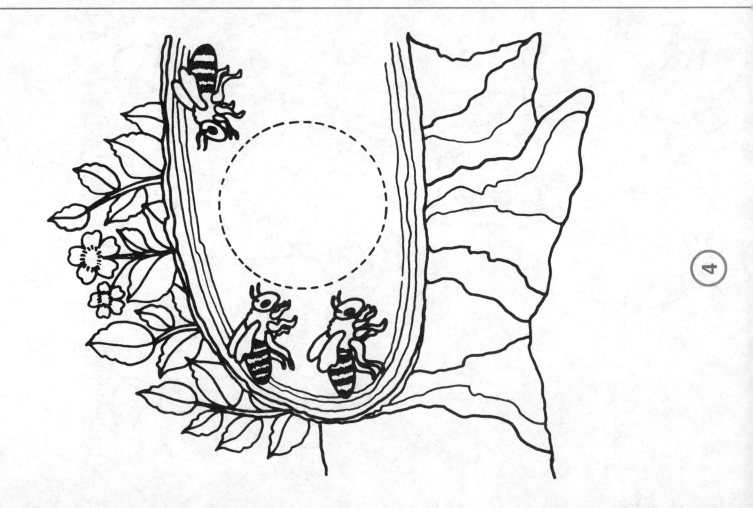

4

Pollen from the blooms

stick to the bees as they go.

They carry it to other flowers

where it helps new fruit grow.

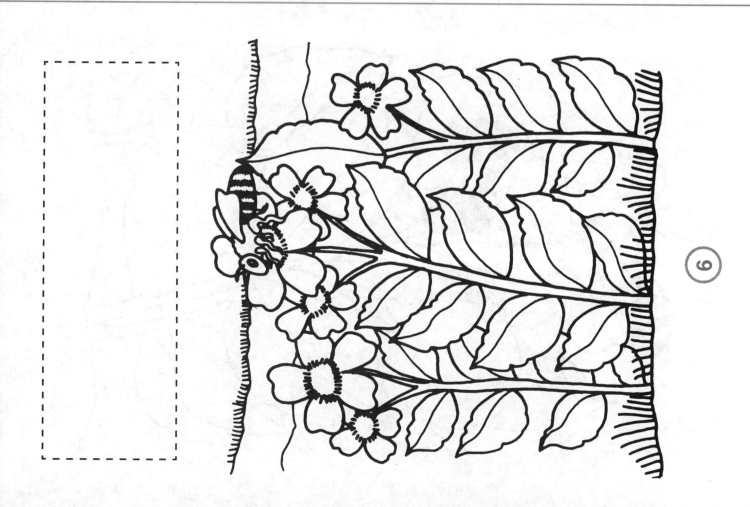

6

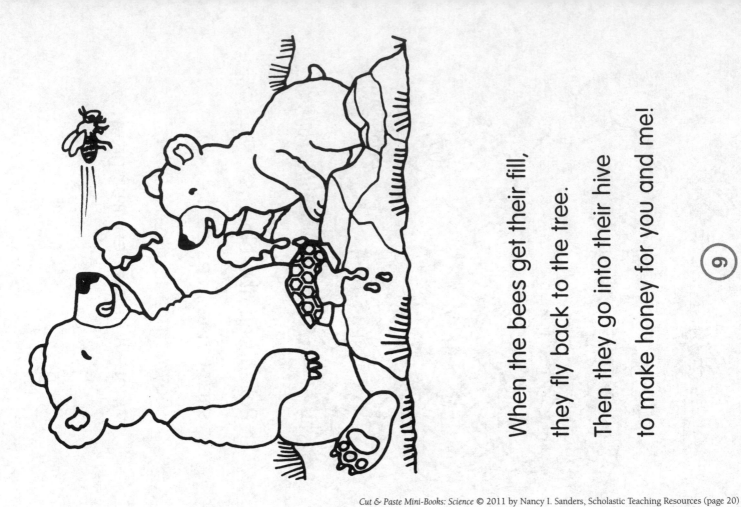

When the bees get their fill,

they fly back to the tree.

Then they go into their hive

to make honey for you and me!

⑨

⑧

Help the bee get to its hive.

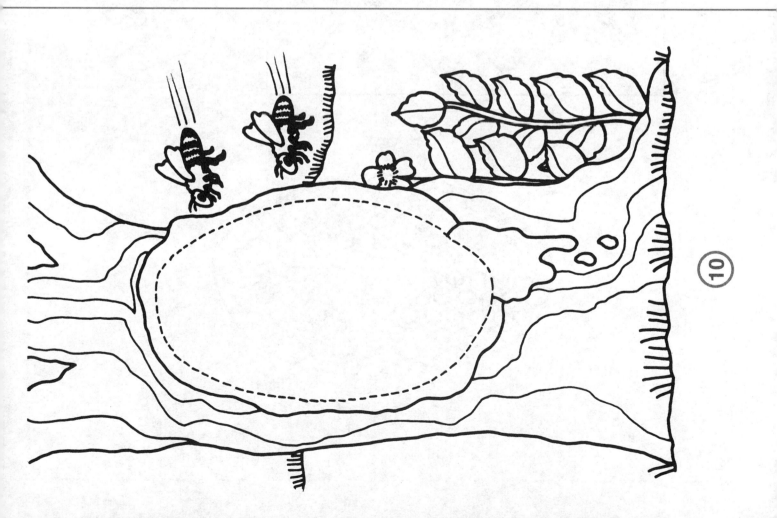

11

Cut & Paste Mini-Books: Science © 2011 by Nancy I. Sanders, Scholastic Teaching Resources (page 21)

10

Busy Bees

Cut & Paste Patterns

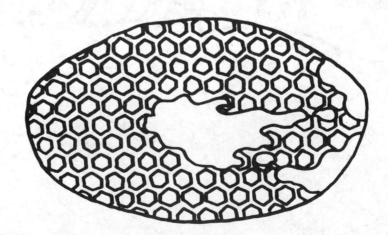

Growing a Garden

Getting Started

Explain that seeds need soil, water, and light to grow into plants. Then work with children to list different kinds of plant seeds. Next, distribute a large seed-shaped paper cutout to each child. (Make each cutout the same size and shape.) Ask children to label their cutout with the name of a seed from the list and then draw a plant, flower, or food that grows from that seed. Bind the pages together to make a class book titled "What Grows From Seeds?"

Completing the Mini-Book

Ask children to write their name on the cover, then cut out and glue the patterns onto the pages, as shown. Finally, have them complete the activity on the last page.

> **Reproducible Pages**
> mini-book:
> pages 24–29
> patterns: page 30

   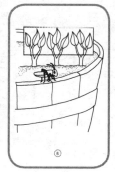  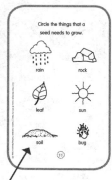

Circle the things that a seed needs to grow.

Taking It Further

To create a class seed collection, give children a few index cards to take home. Instruct them to look for seeds to glue onto the cards (a different seed per card). Have them label each card with the seed name if they know it. If not, they can write "Mystery Seed." In class, examine the seeds with children and name them. If anyone can correctly identify a mystery seed, write its name on the back of the card. Then file the seed cards in a box and keep the collection handy for children to explore during free-choice activities.

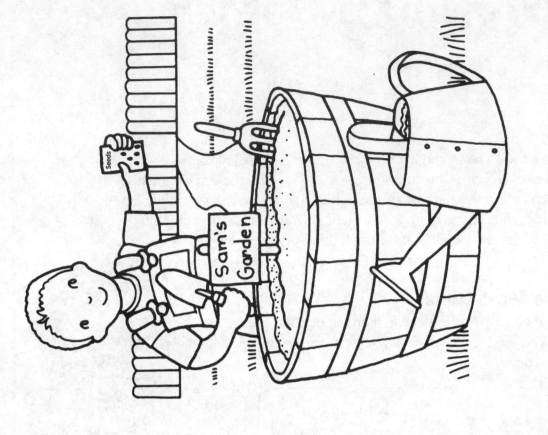

Sam found some seeds.

He decided to plant a garden.

Cut & Paste Mini-Books: Science © 2011 by Nancy I. Sanders, Scholastic Teaching Resources (page 24)

(1)

Growing a Garden

by _____

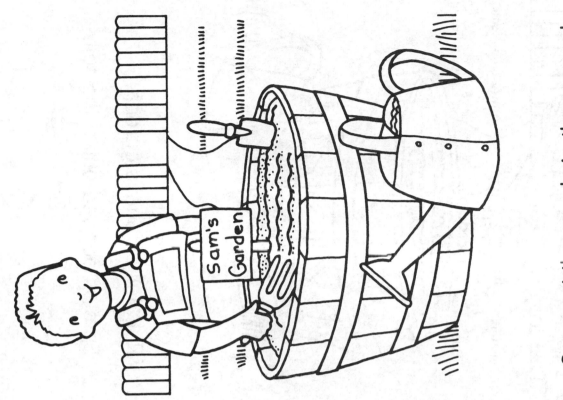

Sam put the seeds in the ground.

He covered them with soil.

③

Cut & Paste Mini-Books: Science © 2011 by Nancy I. Sanders, Scholastic Teaching Resources (page 25)

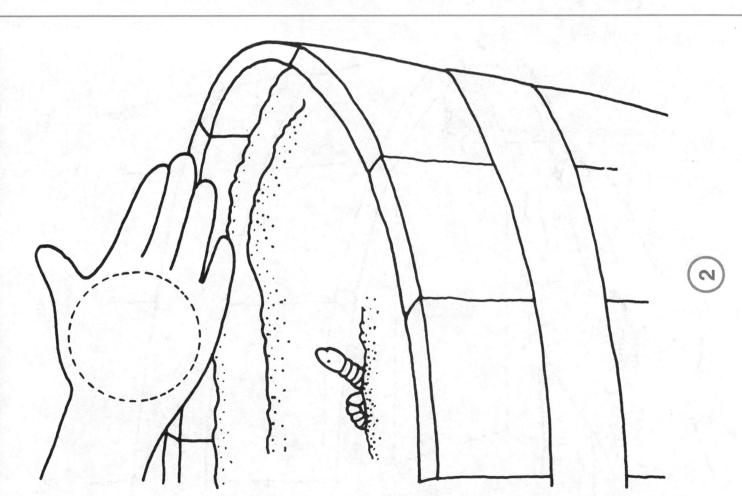

②

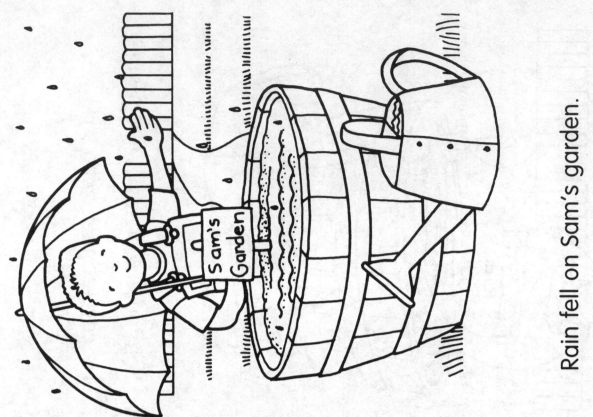

Rain fell on Sam's garden.
Sprouts popped out of the soil.

⑤

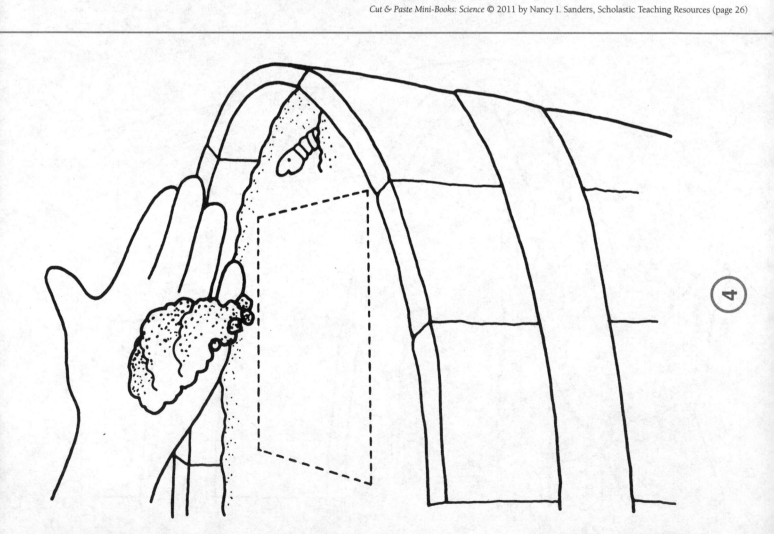

④

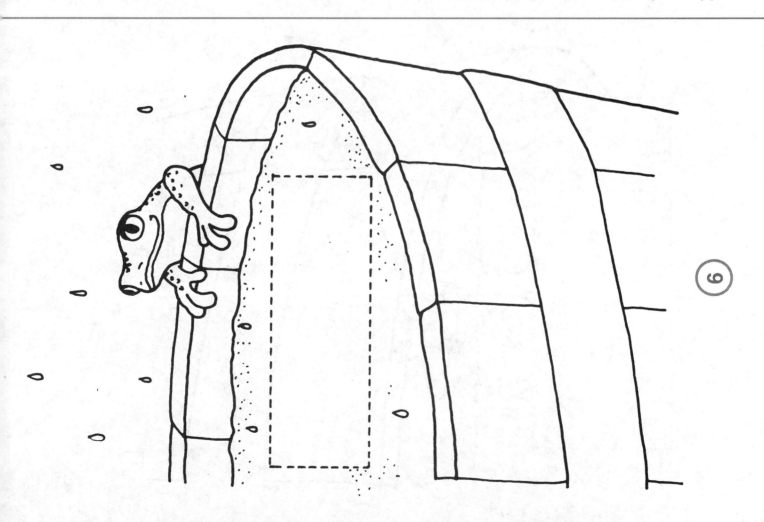

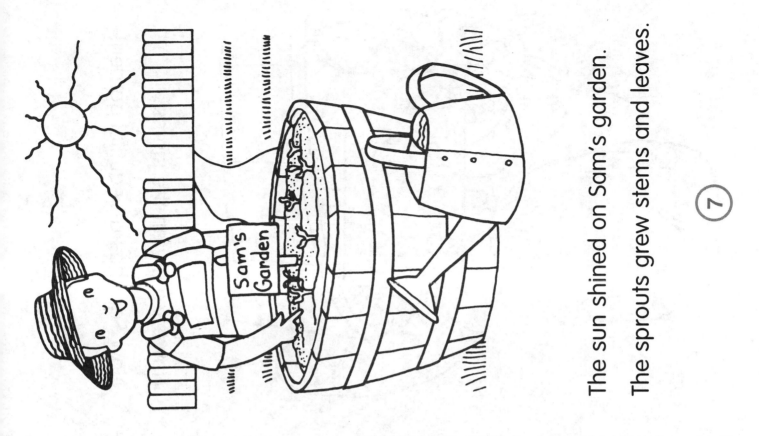

The sun shined on Sam's garden.

The sprouts grew stems and leaves.

⑦

⑥

Flowers grew on the stems.

Now Sam has a beautiful garden!

⑨

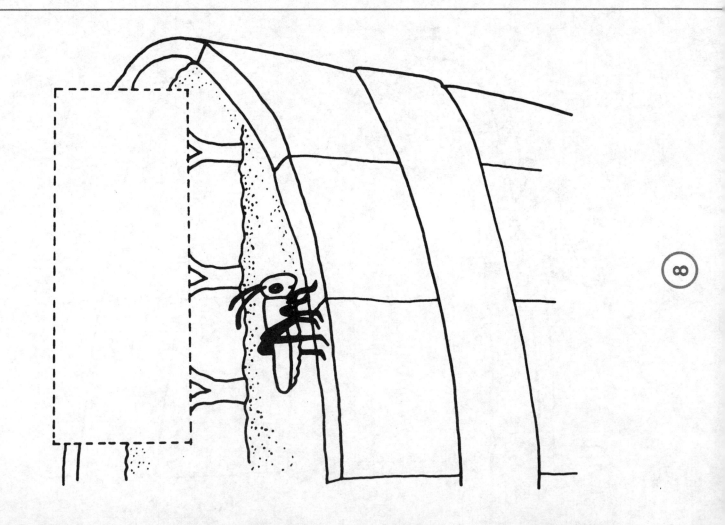

⑧

Circle the things that a
seed needs to grow.

rock

sun

bug

rain

leaf

soil

(11)

Cut & Paste Mini-Books: Science © 2011 by Nancy I. Sanders, Scholastic Teaching Resources (page 29)

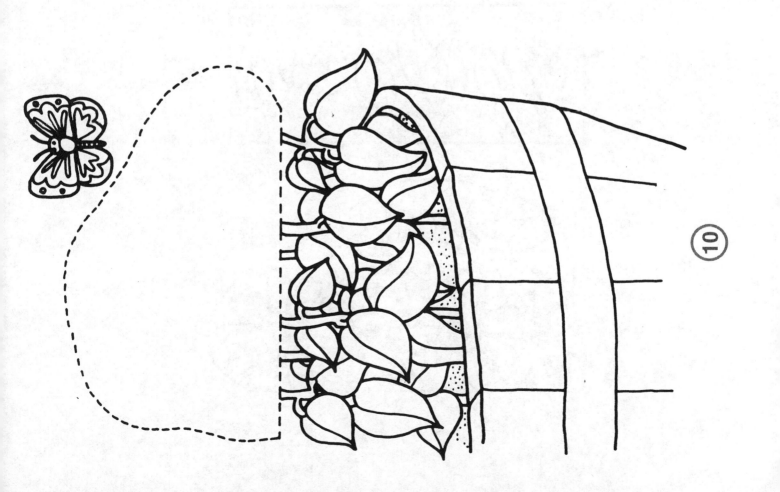

(10)

Growing a Garden

Cut & Paste Patterns

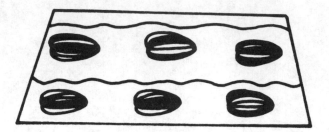

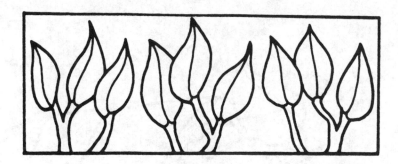

Whose Eggs?

Skill Egg-Laying Animals

Getting Started

Write words related to animals that hatch from eggs on a large egg-shaped cutout. Some words you might include are *egg*, *nest*, *hatch*, *baby*, *duckling*, *snake*, *alligator*, and *chick*. Review the words with children, then display the word bank in the writing center. Add to it as children learn additional egg-related words. Also, encourage children to refer to the word bank when they discuss or write about animals that lay and hatch from eggs.

Completing the Mini-Book

Ask children to write their name on the cover, then cut out and glue the patterns onto the pages, as shown. Finally, have them complete the activity on the last page.

Reproducible Pages
mini-book: pages 32–37
patterns: page 38

Draw an oval around the animals that hatch from eggs.

Taking It Further

Label a four- or five-column chart with the names of pets that hatch from eggs, such as "Bird," "Lizard," "Turtle," and "Snake." You might also include "Other." Then invite children to attach an egg-shaped cutout to each column that represents an egg-hatched pet that they own. (Invite those who don't have pets to place an egg in the column for a pet they would like to own.) When finished, compare and contrast the results. Finally, help children use the results to create a simple line or bar graph.

Duck found four eggs near the water.

"Whose eggs are these?" she cried.

"What baby will come out of each egg?"

Cut & Paste Mini-Books: Science © 2011 by Nancy I. Sanders, Scholastic Teaching Resources (page 32)

Whose Eggs?

by _____

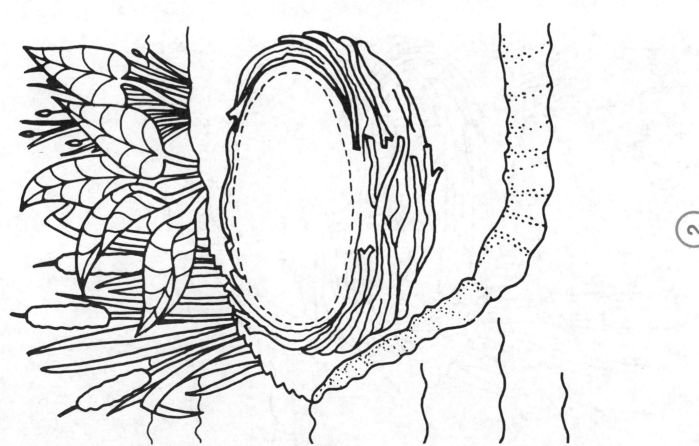

One egg hatches.

Sss! Sss! Sss!

This baby is brown.

It has a shell.

What is it?

③

②

Another egg hatches.

Hiss! Hiss! Hiss!

This baby is red.

Its body looks like a rope.

What is it?

It's a turtle!

Another egg hatches.

Snap! Snap! Snap!

This baby is green.

It has sharp teeth.

What is it?

7

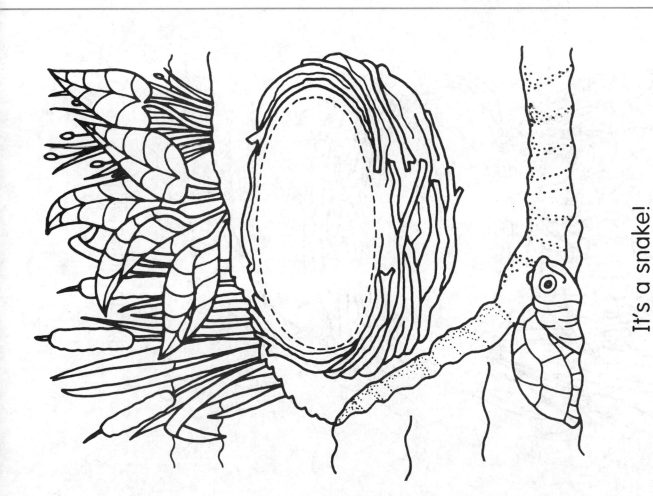

It's a snake!

6

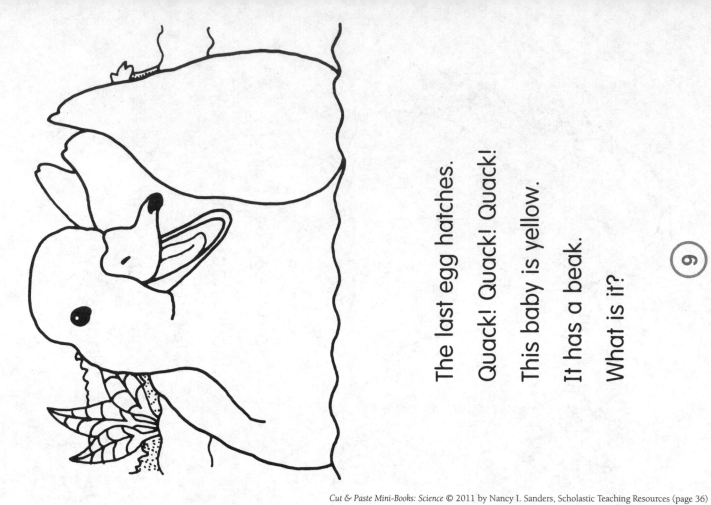

The last egg hatches.

Quack! Quack! Quack!

This baby is yellow.

It has a beak.

What is it?

⑨

Cut & Paste Mini-Books: Science © 2011 by Nancy I. Sanders, Scholastic Teaching Resources (page 36)

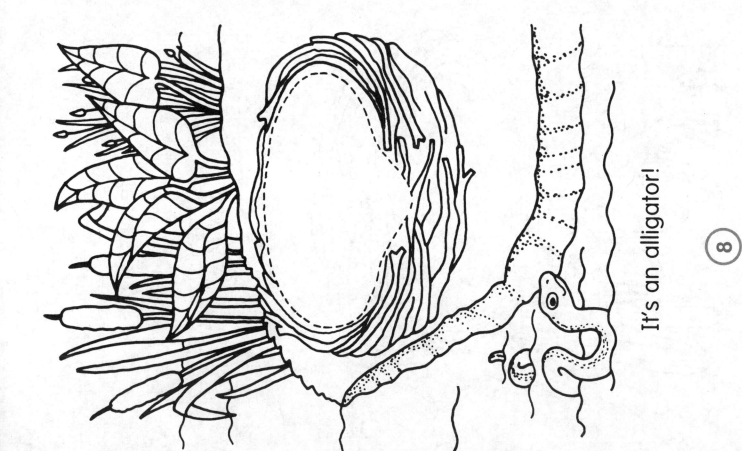

It's an alligator!

⑧

Draw an oval around the animals
that hatch from eggs.

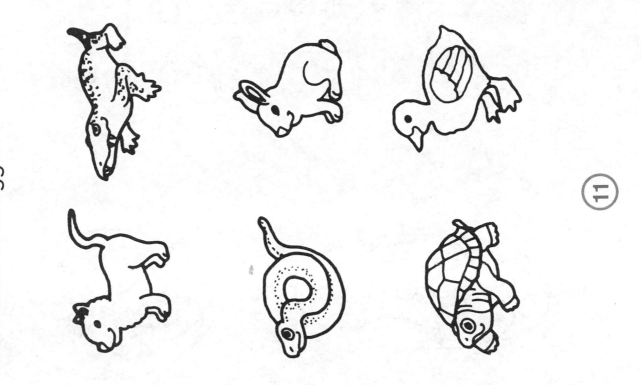

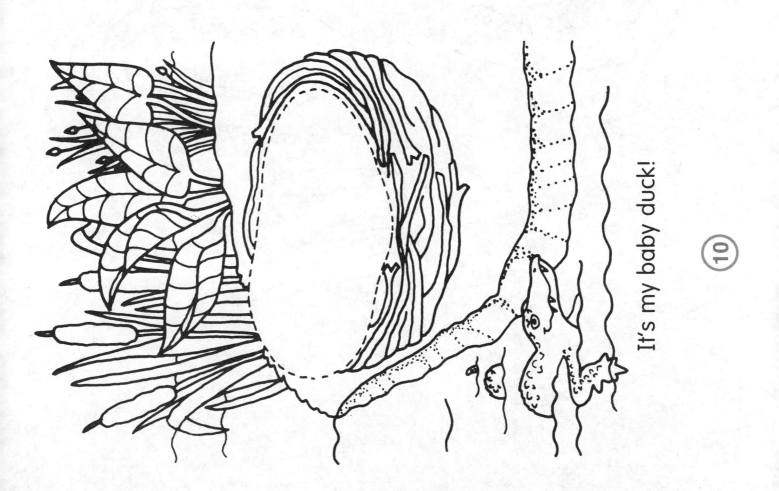

It's my baby duck!

Whose Eggs?

Cut & Paste Patterns

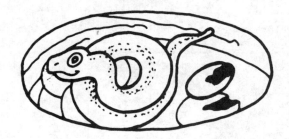

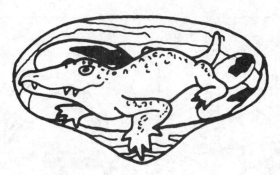

Mama, Where Are You?

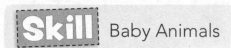

Skill Baby Animals

Getting Started

Explain that many animal babies—such as puppies, kittens, and rabbits—resemble their parents. Ask children to name baby-parent animal pairs that might live on a farm. List their responses, providing the correct name for each animal in a pair, such as *chick/chicken, lamb/sheep, calf/cow,* and *piglet/pig*. Ask children whether or not each baby resembles its parents. Later, write the baby and parent names on separate index cards for children to use in a game of Memory.

Completing the Mini-Book

Ask children to write their name on the cover, then cut out and glue the patterns onto the pages, as shown. Finally, have them complete the activity on the last page.

Reproducible Pages
mini-book: pages 40–45
patterns: pages 46–47

Piglet woke up.
"Mama, where are you?" Piglet cried.
"Oink! Oink!" said Mama Pig.
"I'm here, little one.
And our day has just begun."

Calf woke up.
"Mama, where are you?" Calf cried.
"Moo! Moo!" said Mama Cow
"I'm here, little one.
And our day has just begun."

Lamb woke up.
"Mama, where are you?" Lamb cried.
"Baaa! Baaa!" said Mama Sheep.
"I'm here, little one.
And our day has just begun."

Chick woke up.
"Mama, where are you?" Chick cried.
"Cluck! Cluck!" said Mama Hen.
"I'm here, little one.
And our day has just begun."

Then the mamas and their babies
went outside to play.
They had fun in the barnyard
all throughout the day.

Draw a line from each mama to her baby.

Draw a line from each mama to her baby.

Taking It Further

Punch a hole in each baby-parent card pair from "Getting Started." Attach a length of yarn to each card to make a necklace. Make enough necklaces for each child to have one. (Check that each baby card has a corresponding parent card.) If you have an odd number of children, make an extra baby animal necklace for that child. Distribute the necklaces for children to put on. Then have them try to match the animal on their necklace to the corresponding baby or parent animal on another necklace.

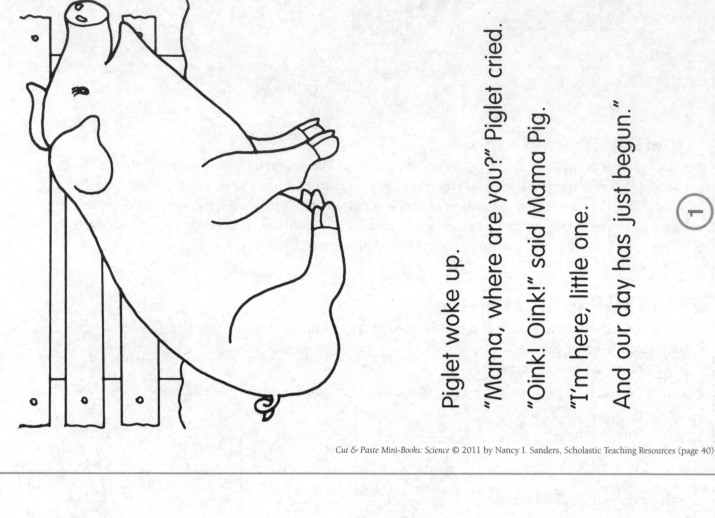

Piglet woke up.

"Mama, where are you?" Piglet cried.

"Oink! Oink!" said Mama Pig.

"I'm here, little one.

And our day has just begun."

Mama, Where Are You?

by _____

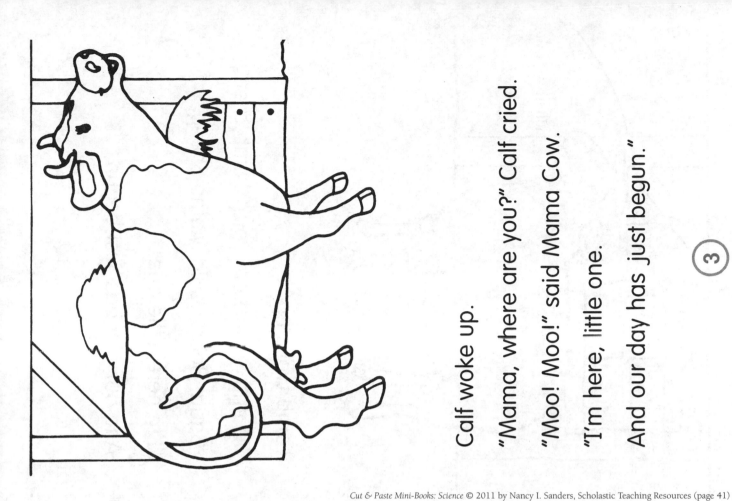

Calf woke up.

"Mama, where are you?" Calf cried.

"Moo! Moo!" said Mama Cow.

"I'm here, little one.

And our day has just begun."

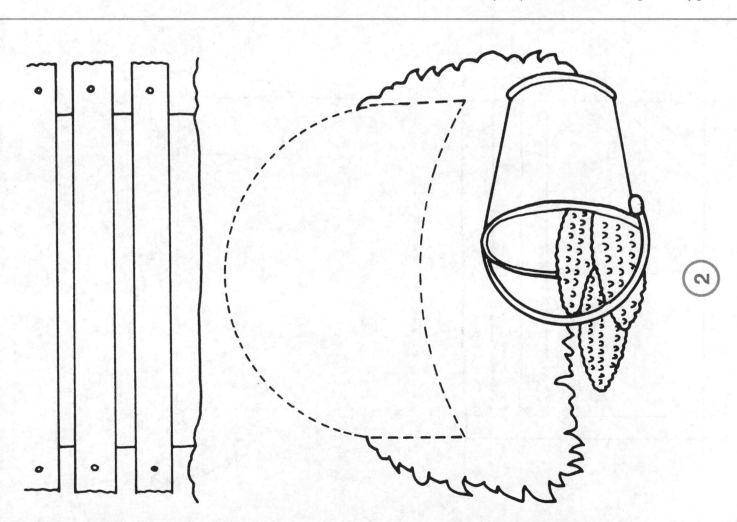

Lamb woke up.

"Mama, where are you?" Lamb cried.

"Baaa! Baaa!" said Mama Sheep.

"I'm here, little one.

And our day has just begun."

⑤

Cut & Paste Mini-Books: Science © 2011 by Nancy I. Sanders, Scholastic Teaching Resources (page 42)

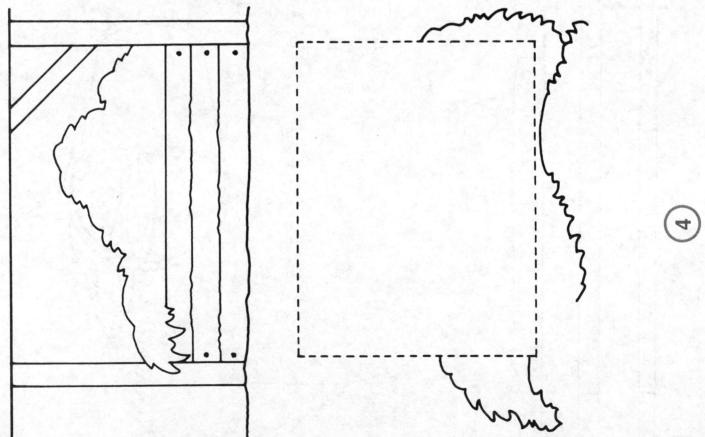

④

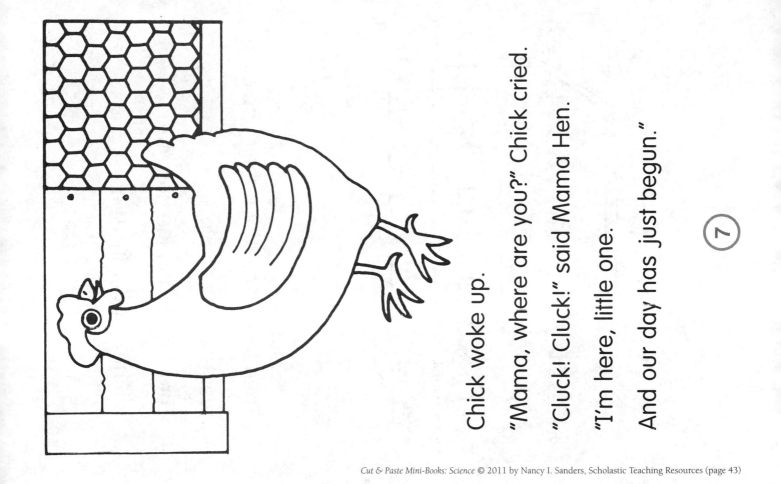

Chick woke up.

"Mama, where are you?" Chick cried.

"Cluck! Cluck!" said Mama Hen.

"I'm here, little one.

And our day has just begun."

(7)

Cut & Paste Mini-Books: Science © 2011 by Nancy I. Sanders, Scholastic Teaching Resources (page 43)

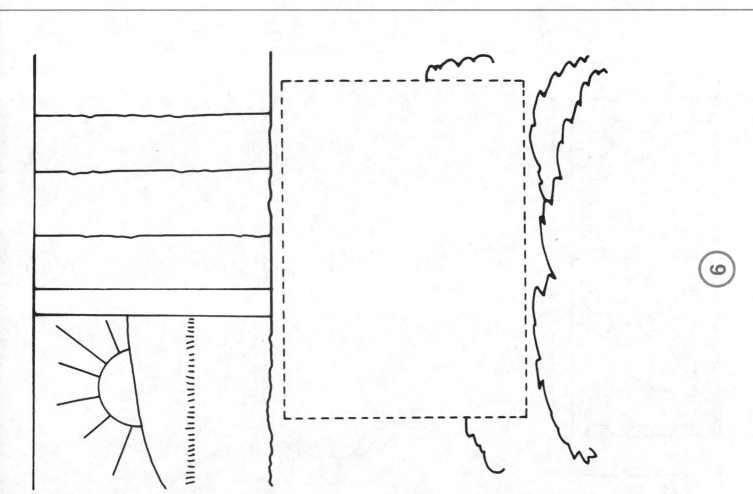

(6)

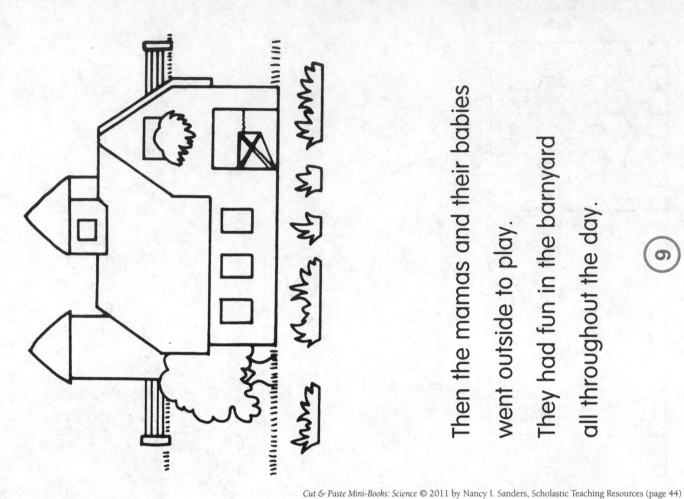

Then the mamas and their babies
went outside to play.
They had fun in the barnyard
all throughout the day.

⑨

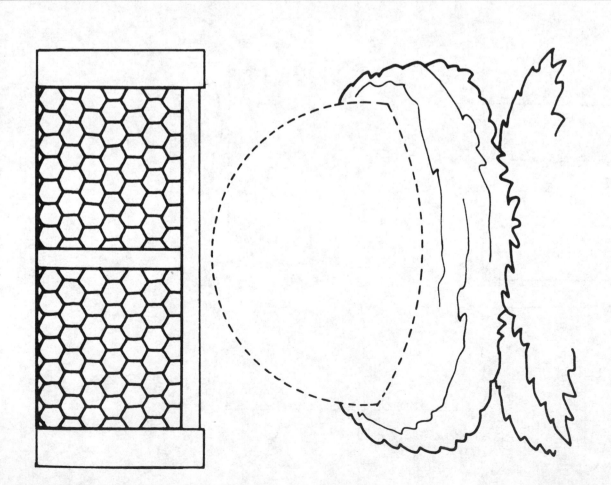

⑧

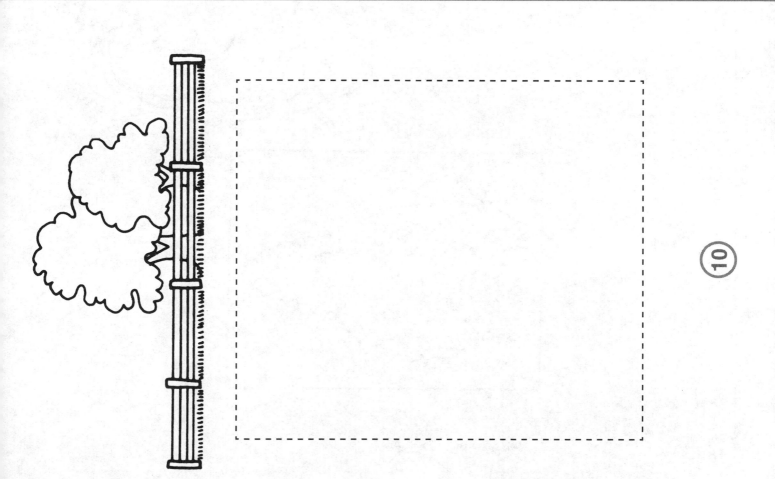

Draw a line from each mama to her baby.

(11)

(10)

Mama, Where Are You?

Cut & Paste Patterns

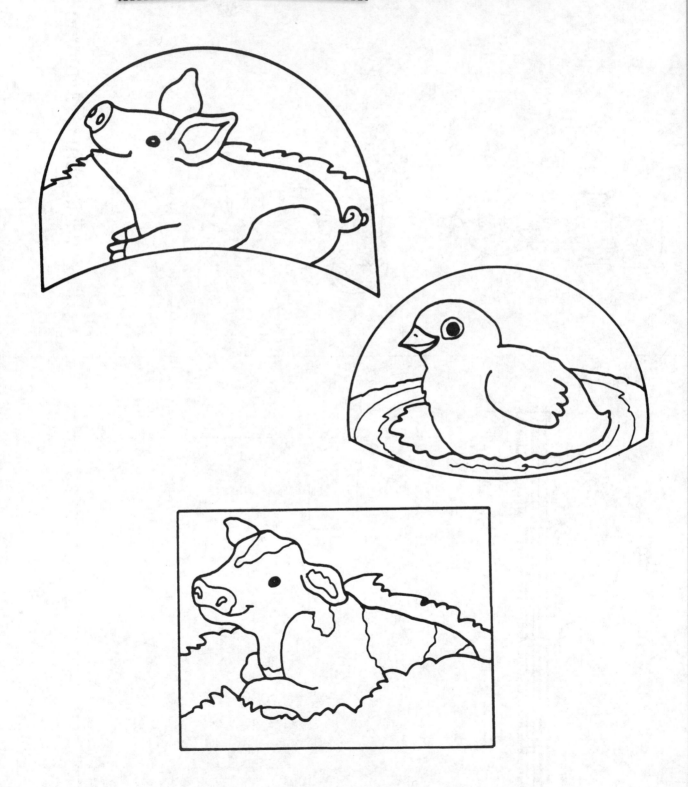

Mama, Where Are You?

Cut & Paste Patterns

Does Frog Live Here?

Getting Started

Work with children to create a list of animal homes, such as *den, anthill, beehive, nest, pond, burrow, dam,* and *shell.* Tell children that these homes provide shelter and security for the animals that live in them. Then point to and name each home on the list. Invite children to name one or more animals that might live in that kind of home and to tell how that home meets the needs of each animal.

Completing the Mini-Book

Ask children to write their name on the cover, then cut out and glue the patterns onto the pages, as shown. Finally, have them complete the activity on the last page.

Reproducible Pages
mini-book:
pages 49–54
patterns: page 55

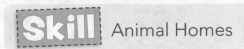

Draw a line from each animal to its home.

Taking It Further

Fill your classroom with pretend animal homes. Be creative! For example, drape a length of dark fabric over a table for a bear den. Set a few child-sized boxes on their sides for groundhog burrows. Provide small rugs or beanbag chairs for bird nests. Use a small plastic swimming pool as a pond and an old crocheted tablecloth as a spider web. Then ask children to pretend to be an animal of their choice. Have them find an appropriate home to settle into. Finally, play a recording of nature sounds as the "animals" rest.

Turtle went to visit Frog.

"Yoo-hoo! Does Frog live here?"

"No!" said Bear. "This is a den.

Only bears live here."

Does Frog Live Here?

by _____

2

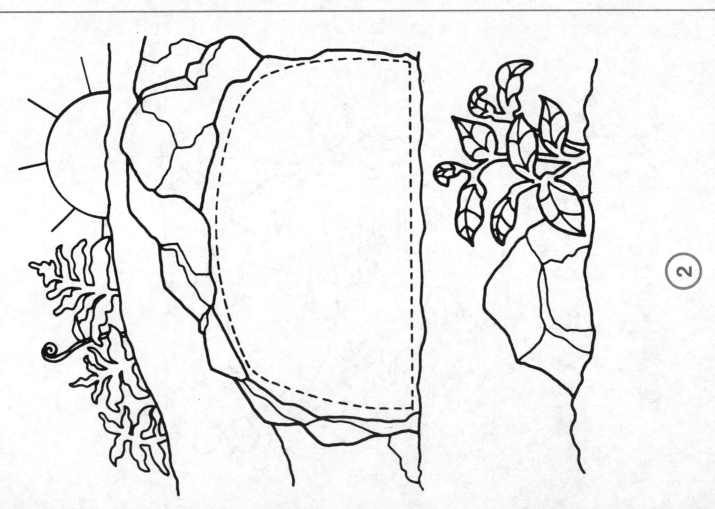

"Yoo-hoo! Does Frog live here?"

"No!" said Ant. "This is an ant hill.

Only ants live here."

3

Cut & Paste Mini-Books: Science © 2011 by Nancy I. Sanders, Scholastic Teaching Resources (page 50)

"Yoo-hoo! Does Frog live here?"

"No!" said Bee. "This is a hive.

Only bees live here."

⑤

④

"Yoo-hoo! Does Frog live here?"

"No!" said Bird. "This is a nest.

Only birds live here."

⑦

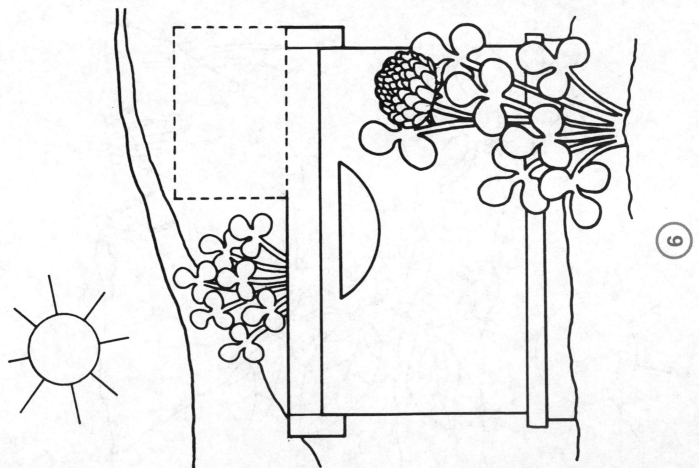

⑥

"Yoo-hoo! Does Frog live here?"

"Yes!" said Frog. "This is a pond.

And I live here!"

"Hooray!" Turtle cheered.

"Now, will you come out and play?"

⑨

⑧

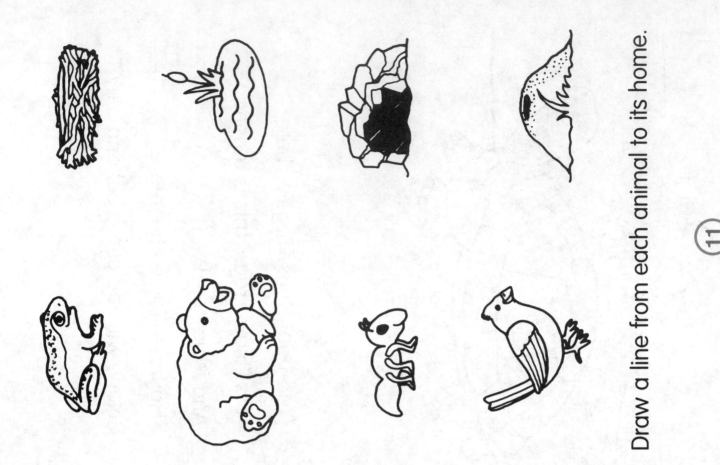

Draw a line from each animal to its home.

11

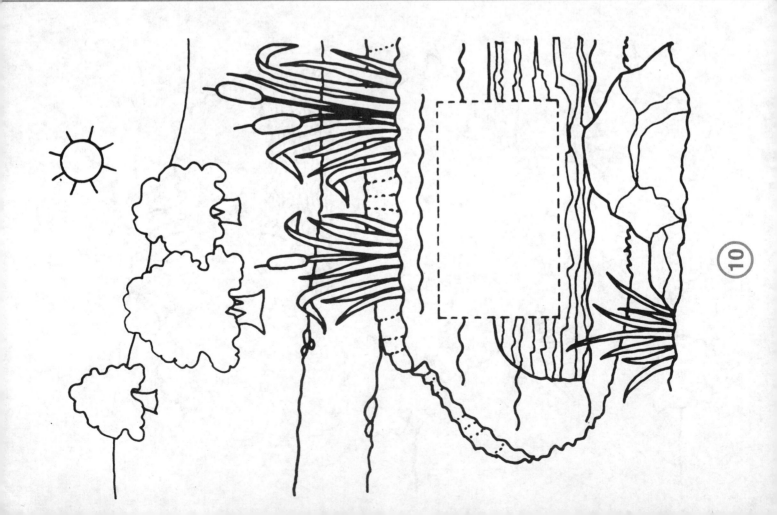

10

Does Frog Live Here?

Cut & Paste Patterns

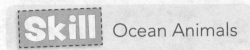

In the Sea

Getting Started

Ask students to name different sea animals. List their responses on chart paper. Also include these animals: *seahorse, goatfish, dogfish, sea lion,* and *whale.* Briefly discuss each animal on the list, inviting children to share what they know about it. Finally, point out that some of the animal names have other animal names hidden in them. Challenge children to find these (such as *goat* in *goatfish* and *horse* in *seahorse*).

Completing the Mini-Book

Ask children to write their name on the cover, then cut out and glue the patterns onto the pages, as shown. Finally, have them complete the activity on the last page.

Reproducible Pages
mini-book: pages 57–62
patterns: page 63

Color the animals that live in the sea.

Taking It Further

Form small groups and assign a sea animal that children may not be very familiar with to each group. Have the groups use the Internet, books, encyclopedias, and other sources to find facts about their animal. Ask each group member to write a fact about the animal on an index card. Then invite the groups to share what they learned about their animal. Allow them to use pictures, if desired. Finally, collect the fact cards, label each with the corresponding animal name, and bind them together with a metal ring. Place the fact cards in your class library.

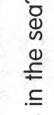

What kind of horse
lives in the sea?

(1)

In the Sea

by _____

What kind of goat
lives in the sea?

③

Cut & Paste Mini-Books: Science © 2011 by Nancy I. Sanders, Scholastic Teaching Resources (page 58)

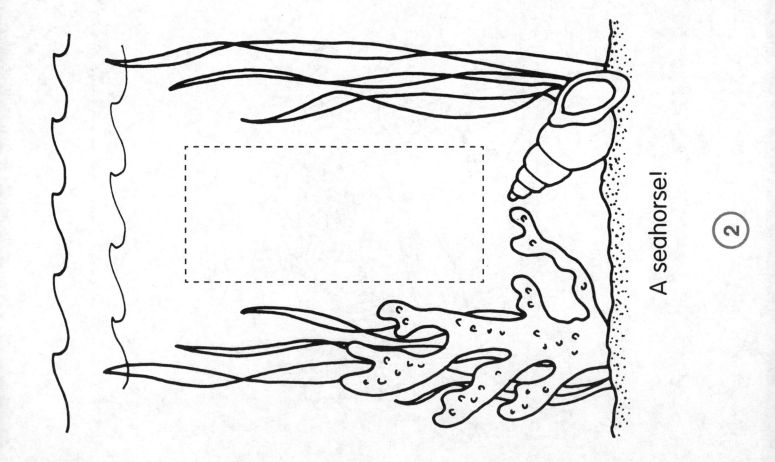

A seahorse!

②

What kind of dog
lives in the sea?

(5)

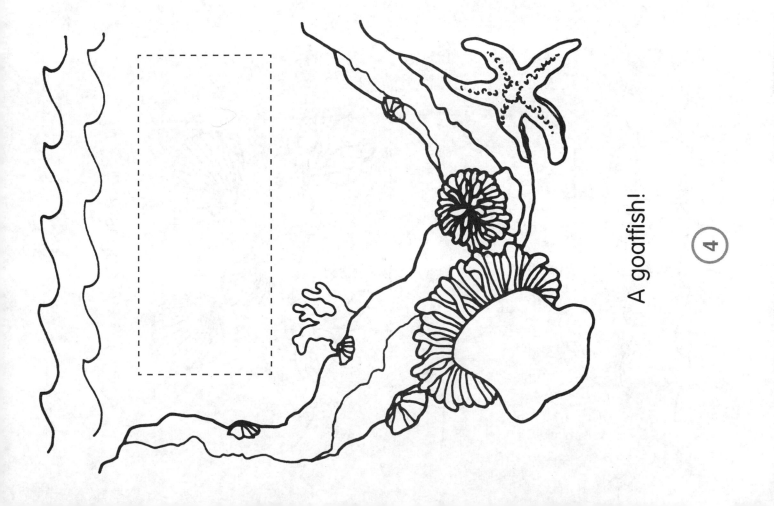

A goatfish!

(4)

What kind of lion
lives in the sea?

⑦

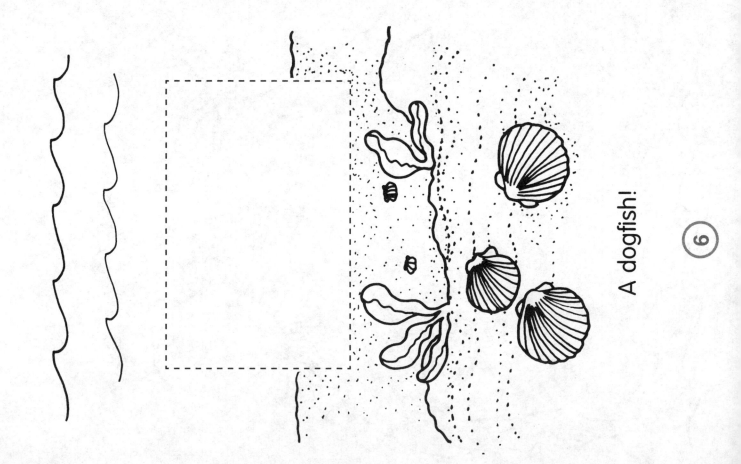

A dogfish!

⑥

What kind of whale

lives in the sea?

⑨

Cut & Paste Mini-Books: Science © 2011 by Nancy I. Sanders, Scholastic Teaching Resources (page 61)

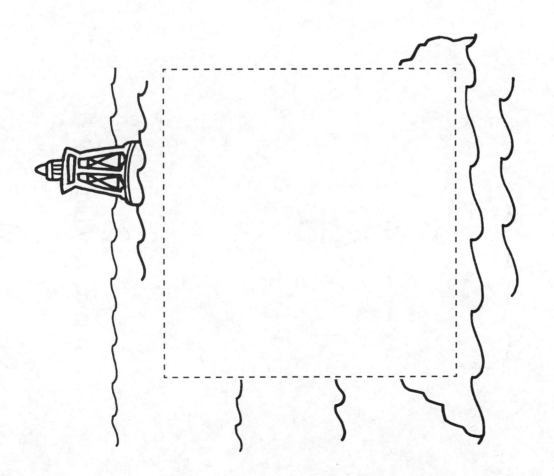

A sea lion!

⑧

Color the animals that live in the sea.

Cut & Paste Mini-Books: Science © 2011 by Nancy I. Sanders, Scholastic Teaching Resources (page 62)

A very, very big one!

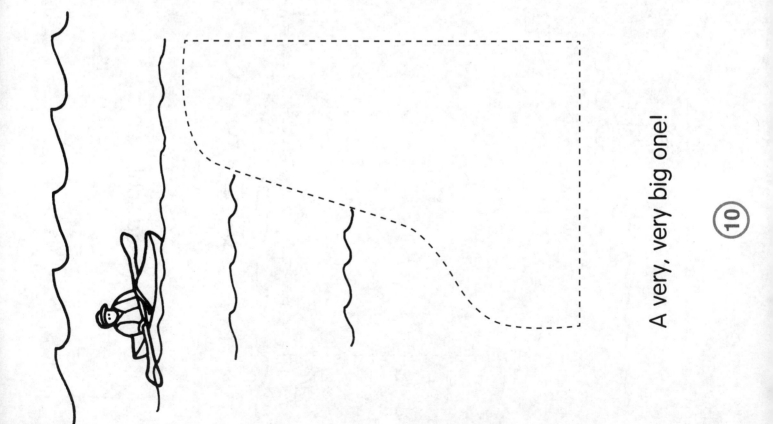

In the Sea

Cut & Paste Patterns

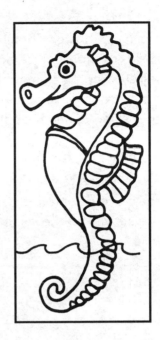

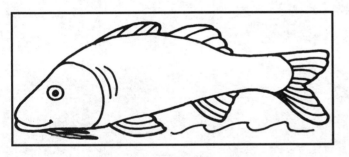

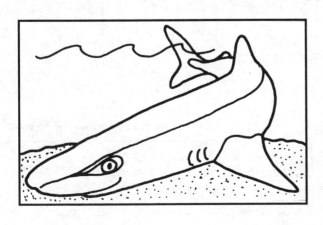

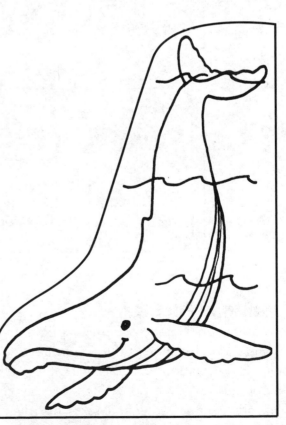

Winter Is Here!

Skill Animals in Winter

Getting Started

What do children do during the winter months? In addition to going to school, do they sled, build snowmen, or ice skate? What do children who live in warmer climates do? After sharing, tell children that different animals do different things during the winter. Explain that some animals, such as geese, *migrate*—they travel to warmer climates. Other animals, such as bears, *hibernate*— they sleep during the cold weather. Still others, like deer, stay awake and active.

Completing the Mini-Book

Ask children to write their name on the cover, then cut out and glue the patterns onto the pages, as shown. Finally, have them complete the activity on the last page.

Reproducible Pages
mini-book:
pages 65–70
patterns: page 71

Connect the dots to reveal the animal.

Taking It Further

Play a game of Hibernation Tag. Appoint one child to be Winter. Ask the other children to pretend to be animals that hibernate, such as bears, skunks, and frogs. On a signal, the animals move about to avoid being tagged by Winter. If Winter tags an animal, it lies down to "hibernate." At any time, Winter may call out "Spring!" as he or she tags an animal. When this happens, the tagged animal takes the role of Winter. Then all of the hibernating animals wake up, and the game continues, this time with the new Winter trying to tag the animals.

Winter is here.

Time to hibernate!

Bear goes to sleep in a den.

Z-z-z-z.

Winter Is Here!

by _____

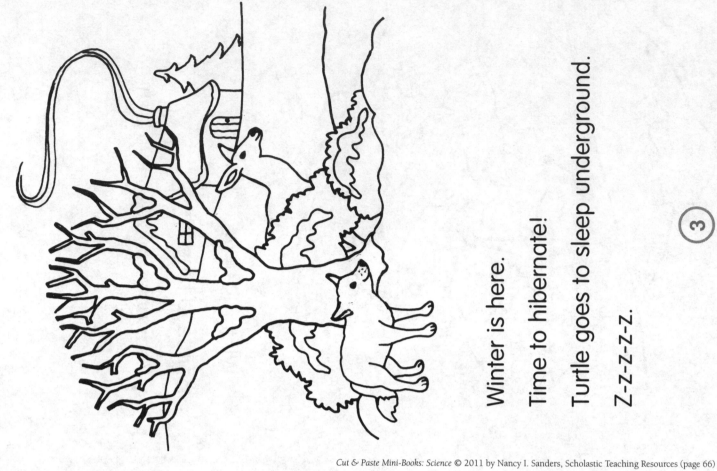

Winter is here.

Time to hibernate!

Turtle goes to sleep underground.

Z-z-z-z.

③

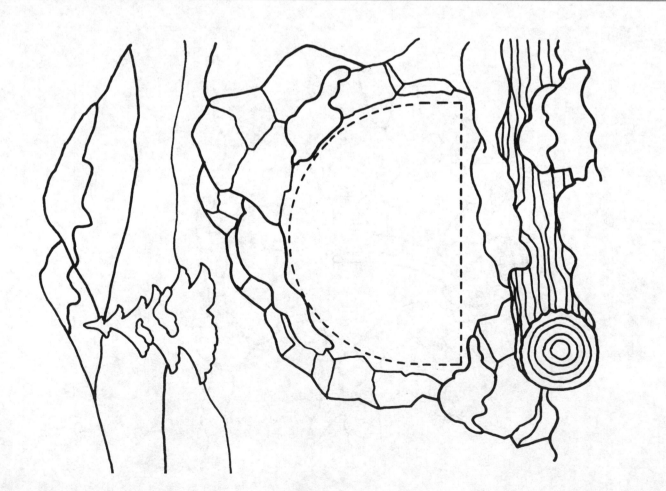

②

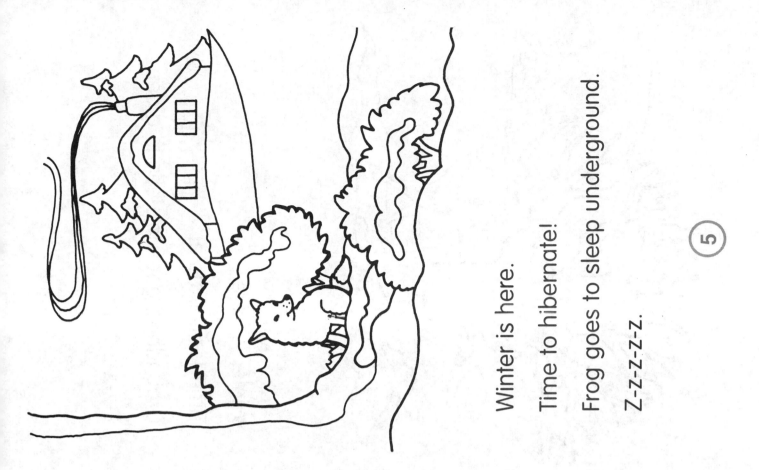

Winter is here.

Time to hibernate!

Frog goes to sleep underground.

Z-z-z-z.

⑤

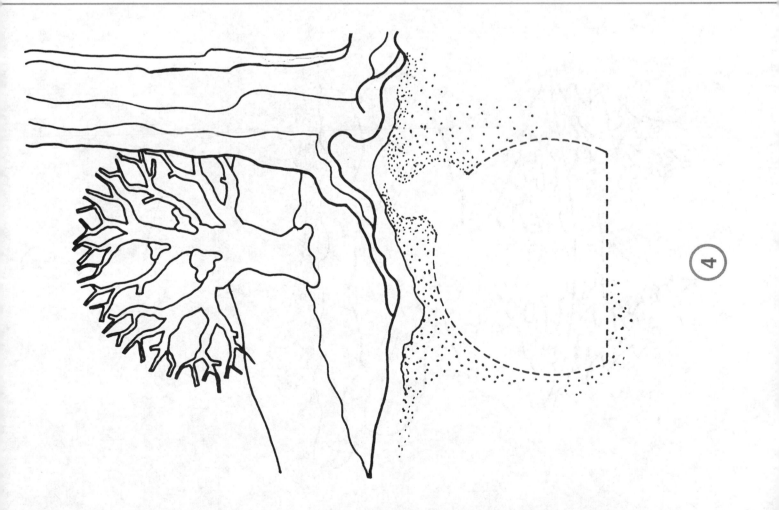

④

Winter is here.

Time to hibernate!

Groundhog goes to sleep in a den.

Z-z-z-z.

(7)

(6)

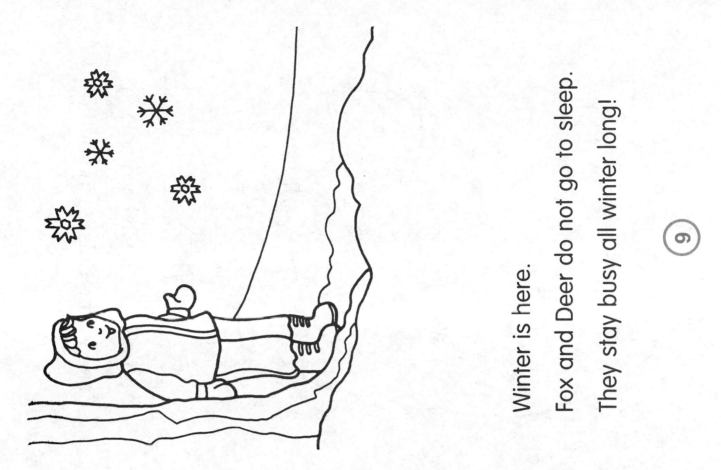

Winter is here.

Fox and Deer do not go to sleep.

They stay busy all winter long!

⑨

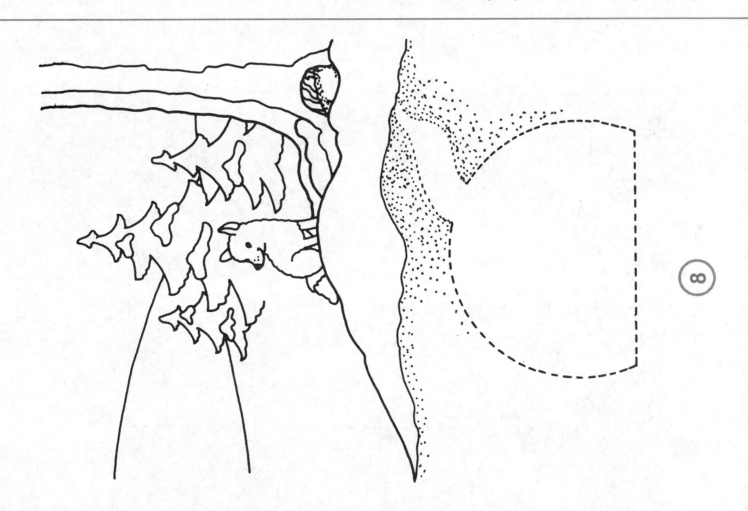

⑧

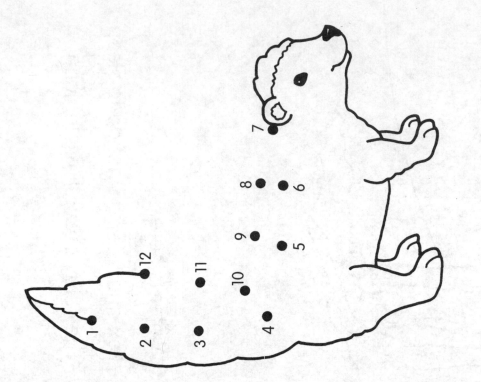

Who else sleeps all winter long?
Connect the dots to find out!

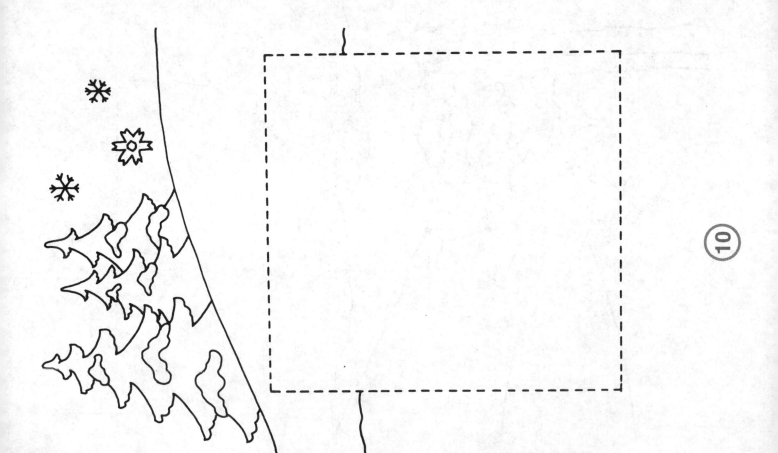

Winter Is Here!

Cut & Paste Patterns

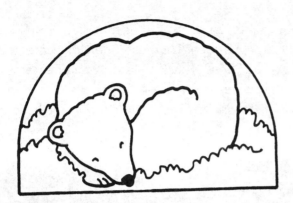

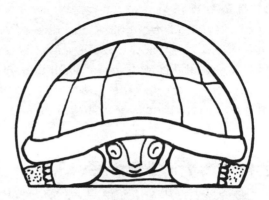

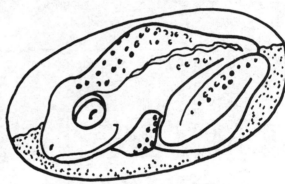

The Fair

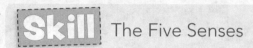

Getting Started

Divide a display into five sections and title it "What Can I _____?" Label each of five large index cards with one of the following: *See, Hear, Smell, Taste,* or *Touch.* Then use one word card at a time to complete the question (for example, "What Can I See?"). Ask children to name items in the classroom to answer the question. List their responses in a section on the display, then attach the corresponding word card to that section. Later, invite children to draw items from each list to add to the display.

Completing the Mini-Book

Ask children to write their name on the cover, then cut out and glue the patterns onto the pages, as shown. Finally, have them complete the activity on the last page.

> **Reproducible Pages**
> mini-book: pages 73–78
> patterns: page 79

Circle the things you can taste.

Taking It Further

Seat children in a circle and have them imagine they went to the fair. Then complete this sentence frame with an item from your imaginary experience: "At the fair, I tasted a ..." (hot dog, for example). Have the next player repeat your sentence and add to it. For instance, "At the fair, I tasted a hot dog and fries." Continue around the circle, inviting each player to add to the sentence. If a player repeats the sentence incorrectly, or is unable to add a new item, the round ends. Then that child starts a new round, using a different sentence frame, such as "At the fair, I smelled a ..."

On Saturday,

I went to the fair.

I tasted many things.

The cotton candy was my favorite.

The Fair

by _____

I smelled many things.

The popcorn was my favorite.

③

Cut & Paste Mini-Books: Science © 2011 by Nancy I. Sanders, Scholastic Teaching Resources (page 74)

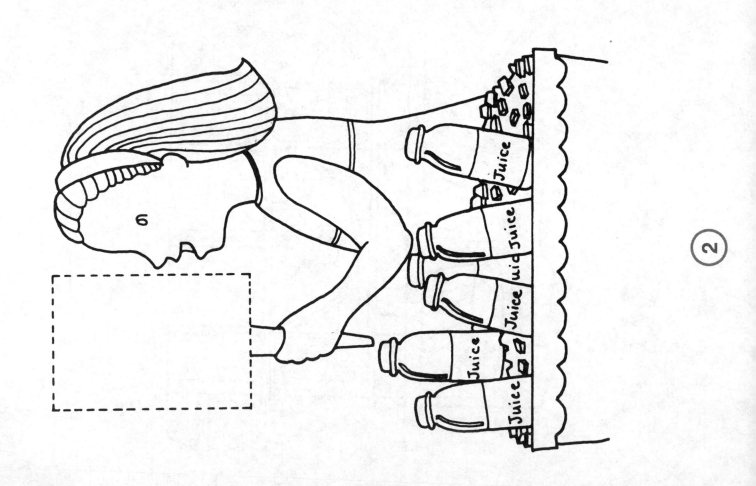

②

I saw many things.

The pig races were my favorite.

⑤

Cut & Paste Mini-Books: Science © 2011 by Nancy I. Sanders, Scholastic Teaching Resources (page 75)

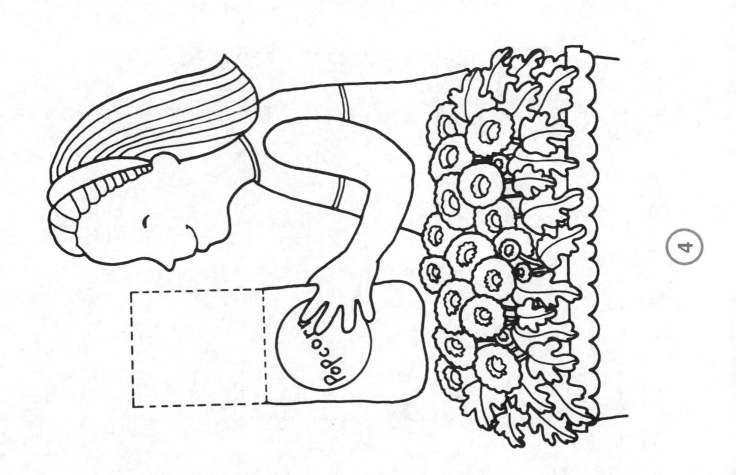

④

I heard many things.

The drum was my favorite.

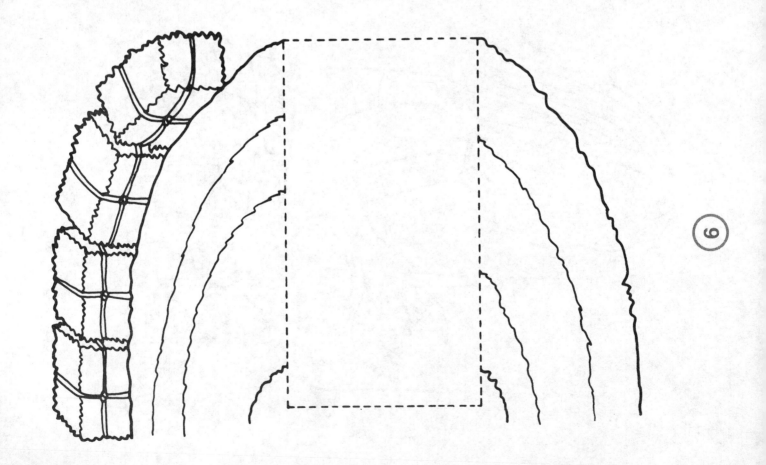

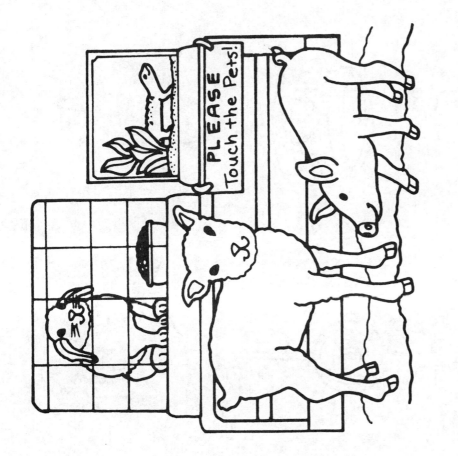

I touched many things.

The rabbit was my favorite.

Dad said I could buy it.

Now I have a pet of my own!

⑨

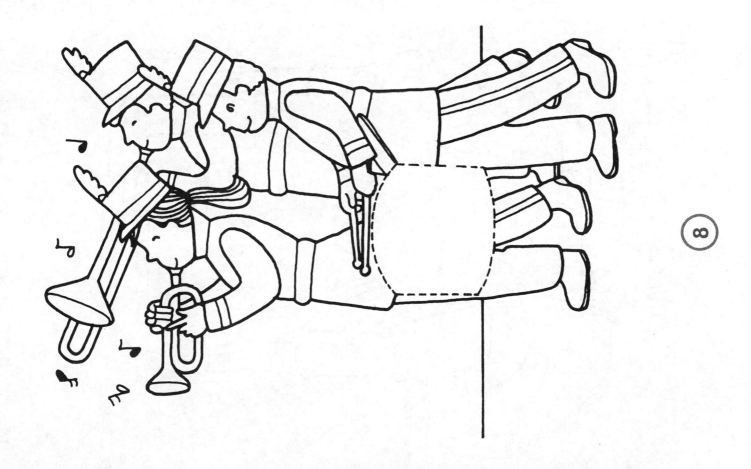

⑧

Circle the things you can taste.

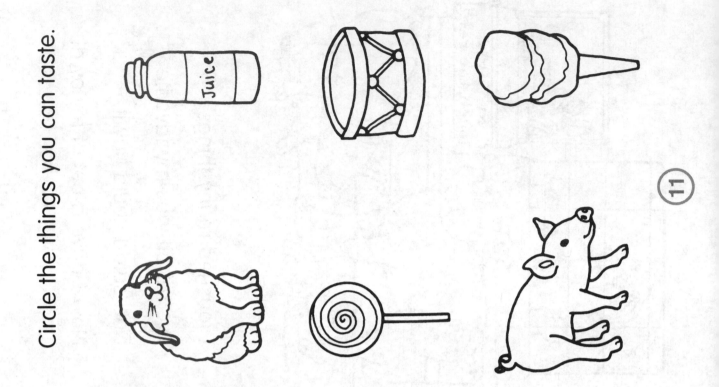

(11)

Welcome to the Fair

TICKETS

Live Pig

(10)

The Fair

Cut & Paste Patterns

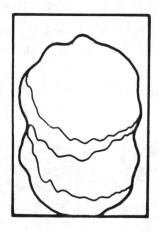

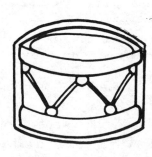

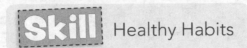

I Make Healthy Choices

Getting Started

Ask children to tell about things they can do to stay healthy, such as washing their hands, exercising, eating nutritious foods, getting plenty of rest, and dressing appropriately for the weather. As you talk about each healthy behavior, also include how that behavior might help others stay healthy (for instance, hand washing helps keep germs from spreading).

Completing the Mini-Book

Ask children to write their name on the cover, then cut out and glue the patterns onto the pages, as shown. Finally, have them complete the activity on the last page.

Reproducible Pages
mini-book: pages 81–86
patterns: page 87

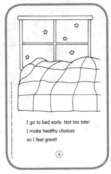

Circle the pictures that show healthy choices that you make.

Taking It Further

Help children get into the habit of washing their hands. First, title a display "We Wash Our Hands." Then have children trace around one of their hands, cut it out along the outline, and write their name on it. Attach the cutouts to the display and place a supply of removable sticker dots nearby. To use, invite children to put a sticker dot on their cutout each time they wash their hands. At the end of the day, have children count their stickers and then remove them to prepare the display for the next day.

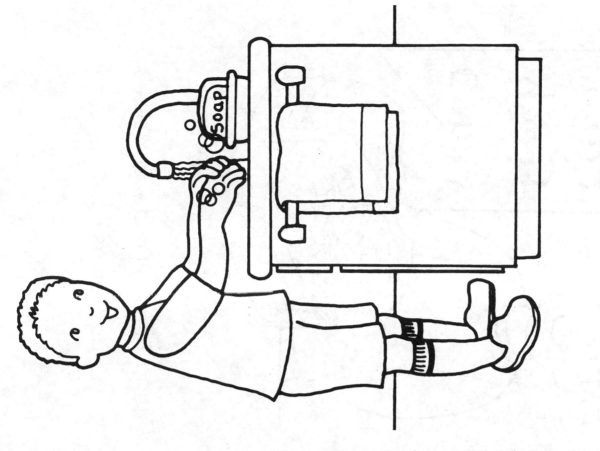

I use soap to wash my hands.

(1)

Cut & Paste Mini-Books: Science © 2011 by Nancy I. Sanders, Scholastic Teaching Resources (page 81)

I Make Healthy Choices

☐ Wash hands
☐ Eat right.
☐ Exercise.
☐ Get lots of sleep!

by

Farm Fresh Foods

I eat fruit and vegetables
as often as I can.

③

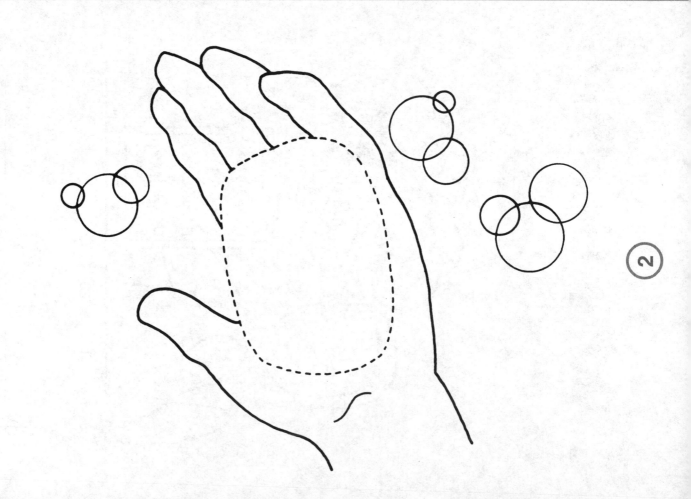

②

I play outside after school.

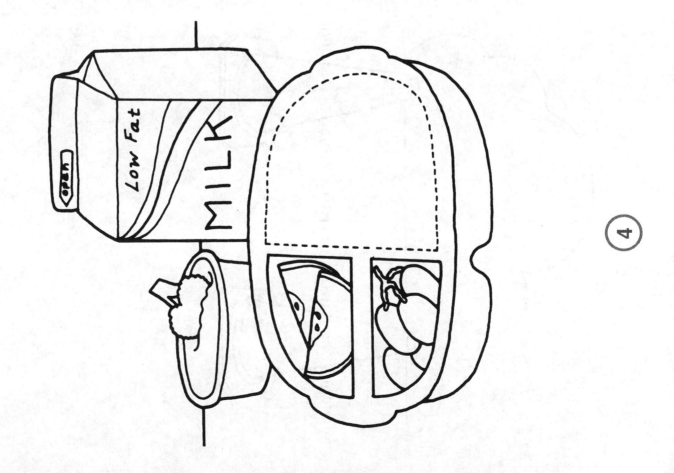

Low Fat
MILK
Open

I wear a hat
when the weather is cool.

⑦

Cut & Paste Mini-Books: Science © 2011 by Nancy I. Sanders, Scholastic Teaching Resources (page 84)

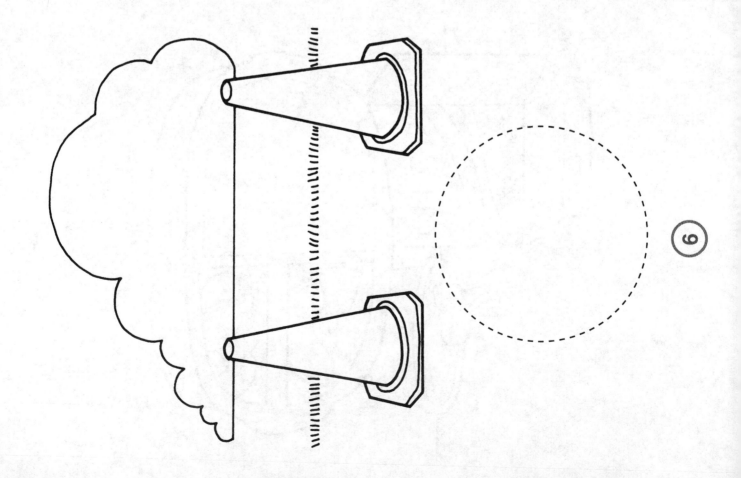

⑥

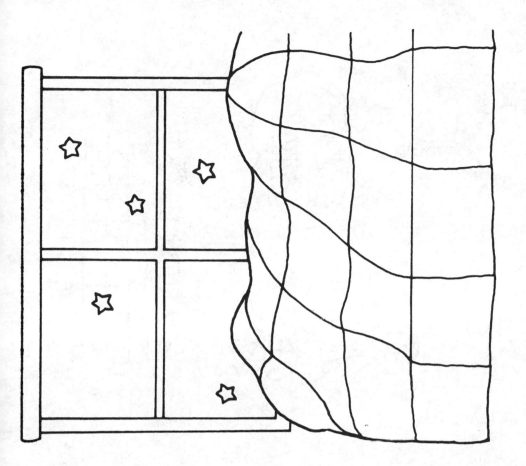

I go to bed early. Not too late!

I make healthy choices

so I feel great!

⑨

⑧

Circle the pictures that show healthy choices that you make.

11

10

I Make Healthy Choices

Cut & Paste Patterns

Piggy Potluck

Skill Nutrition

Getting Started

Download and print a color copy of the *My Pyramid for Kids* poster for ages 6–11 (www.mypyramid.gov/tips_resources/printmaterials.html). Display the poster, then point out one food group at a time. Ask children to name foods that are pictured for that group, as well as other foods that belong to it. Use the information on the poster as a guide to discuss additional information about the food groups, including recommended daily servings.

Completing the Mini-Book

Ask children to write their name on the cover, then cut out and glue the patterns onto the pages, as shown. Finally, have them complete the activity on the last page.

Reproducible Pages
mini-book: pages 89–94
patterns: page 95

Draw three healthy foods on the plate.

Taking It Further

Cover each of five flip-top shoeboxes with orange, green, red, blue, or purple paper and label them to represent the major food groups on the food pyramid. Then distribute large index cards to children. Have them write their name on one side and draw a picture of their favorite healthy food on the other side. When finished, invite children to share their drawing and tell the class about it. Finally, have them put the card in the corresponding food group box. Later, put the cards and boxes in a center for children to use for a sorting activity.

This little piggy likes pasta.

Cut & Paste Mini-Books: Science © 2011 by Nancy I. Sanders, Scholastic Teaching Resources (page 89)

Piggy Potluck

You're Invited to a
Piggy Party
and Pot luck

Day: Saturday

Time: 12:00

Don't Forget to:
wear a costume and
bring a healthy food
to share!

by _____

This little piggy likes beans.

③

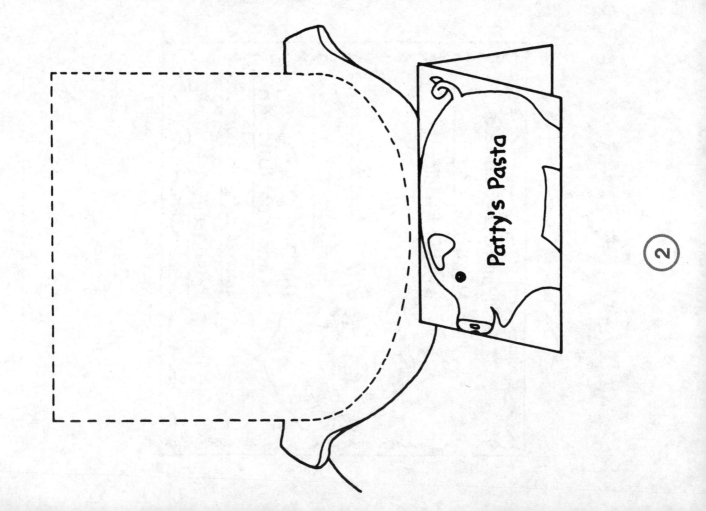

Patty's Pasta

②

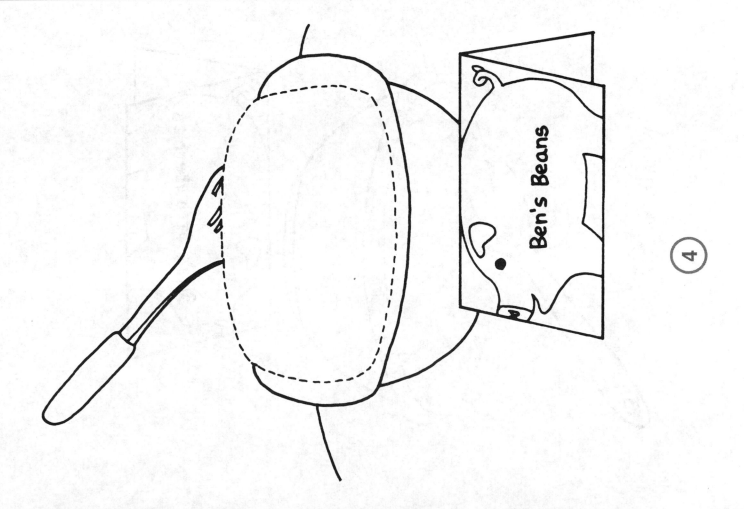

④

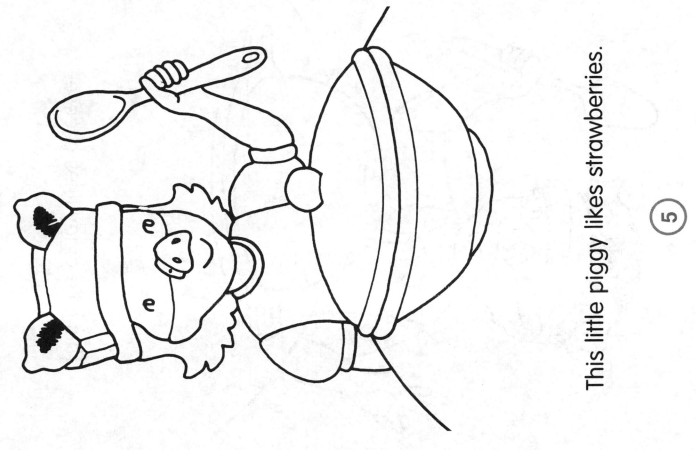

This little piggy likes strawberries.

⑤

Cut & Paste Mini-Books: Science © 2011 by Nancy I. Sanders, Scholastic Teaching Resources (page 91)

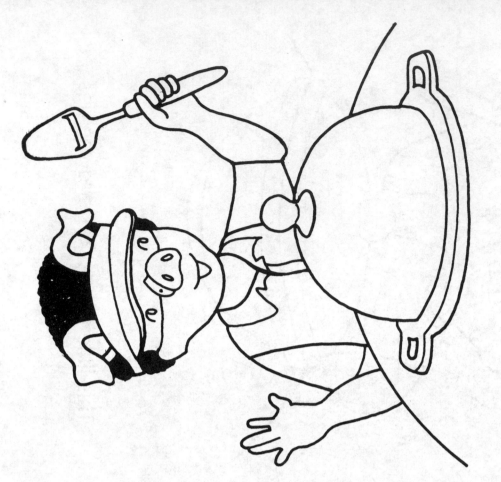

This little piggy likes cheese.

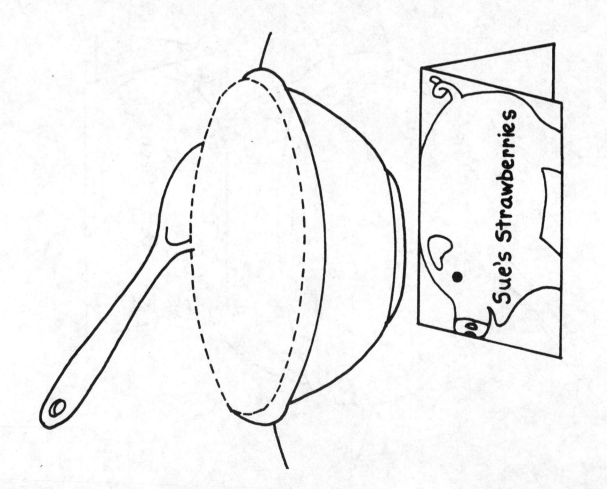

Sue's Strawberries

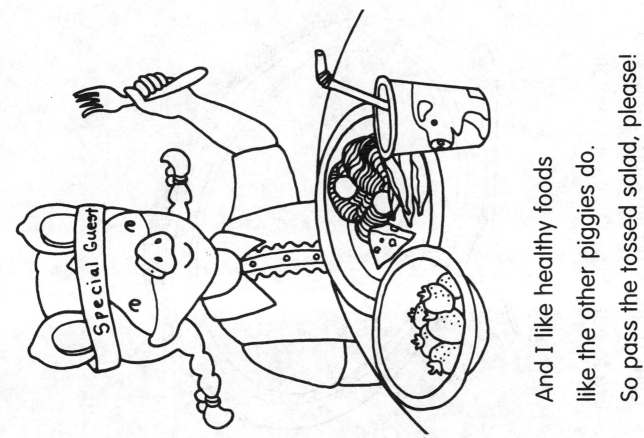

And I like healthy foods

like the other piggies do.

So pass the tossed salad, please!

⑨

Cut & Paste Mini-Books: Science © 2011 by Nancy I. Sanders, Scholastic Teaching Resources (page 93)

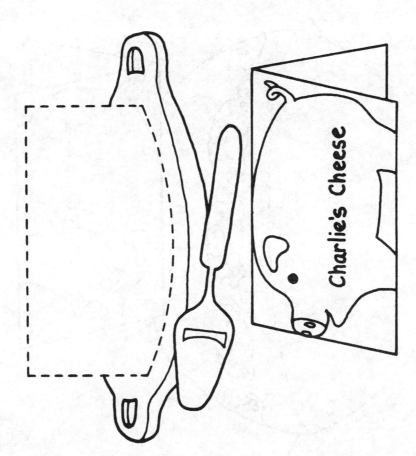

Charlie's Cheese

⑧

Think of three healthy foods that you
like to eat. Draw them on the plate.

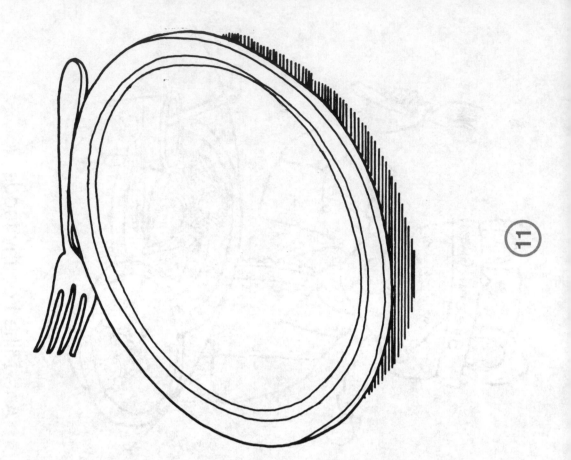

Cut & Paste Mini-Books: Science © 2011 by Nancy I. Sanders, Scholastic Teaching Resources (page 94)

11

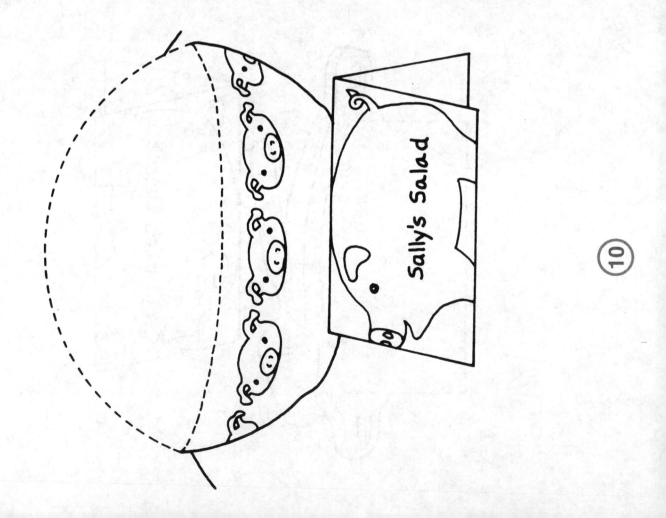

Sally's Salad

10

Piggy Potluck

Cut & Paste Patterns

Molly's Teeth

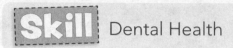

Skill Dental Health

Getting Started

Do children brush their teeth every day? Ask for a show of hands to find out. Then engage children in a discussion about taking care of their teeth. What do they use to clean their teeth? Do they rinse after brushing? Do they floss or use mouthwash? Talk about how and why different items (toothbrush, floss) and products (toothpaste, mouthwash) can help children keep their teeth and mouth healthy.

Completing the Mini-Book

Ask children to write their name on the cover, then cut out and glue the patterns onto the pages, as shown. Finally, have them complete the activity on the last page.

Reproducible Pages
mini-book:
pages 97–102
patterns:
page 103

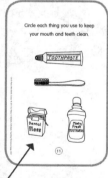

Circle each thing you use to keep your mouth and teeth clean.

Taking It Further

Cut out a class supply of a large tooth shape from white construction paper. Distribute the cutouts to children. Have them write their name and draw a happy face on their cutout. Then display all of the cutouts on a bulletin board, placing a basket of star stickers nearby. To use, invite children to affix a star to their tooth cutout on each day that they clean their teeth. When children collect 10 stars (or any other number you'd like to use), invite them to choose a reward, such as a new toothbrush, a small toy, or extra free-choice time.

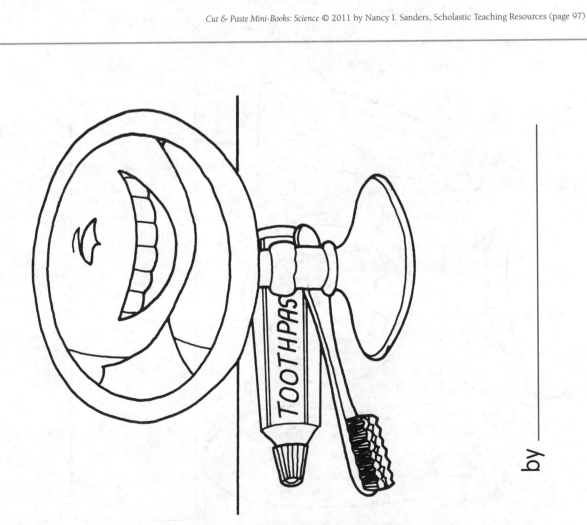

Molly used a toothbrush
to brush her teeth.

Molly's Teeth

by _____

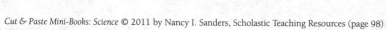

Molly used floss
to clean between her teeth.

(3)

Cut & Paste Mini-Books: Science © 2011 by Nancy I. Sanders, Scholastic Teaching Resources (page 98)

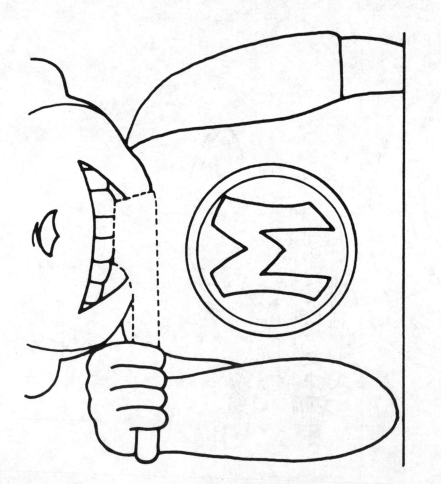

(2)

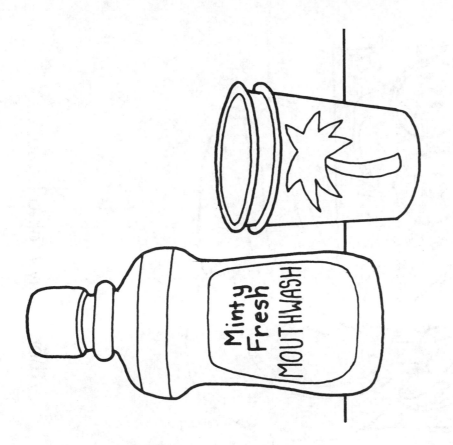

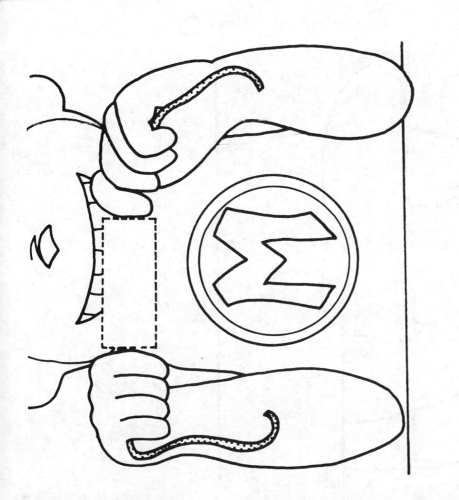

Molly used mouthwash
to rinse her mouth.

Cut & Paste Mini-Books: Science © 2011 by Nancy I. Sanders, Scholastic Teaching Resources (page 99)

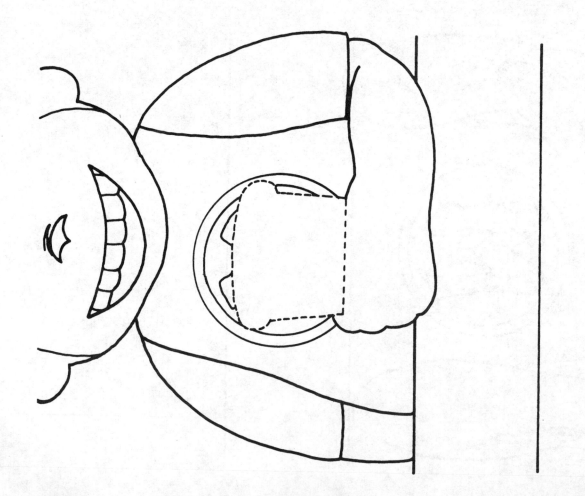

Then Molly took a banana.

6

Surprise! Molly is a monkey!

But she takes care of her teeth

just like you do!

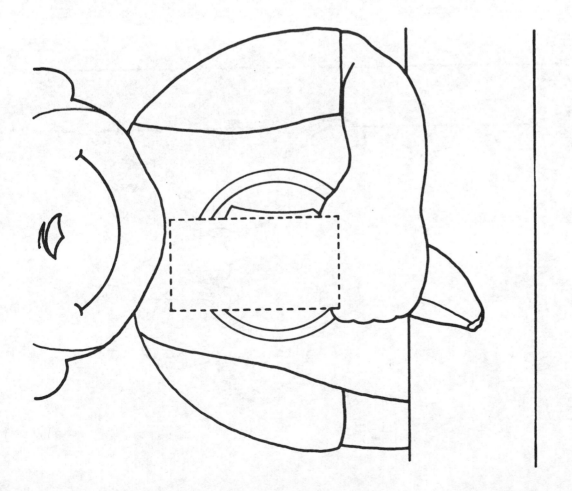

Circle each thing you use to keep your mouth and teeth clean.

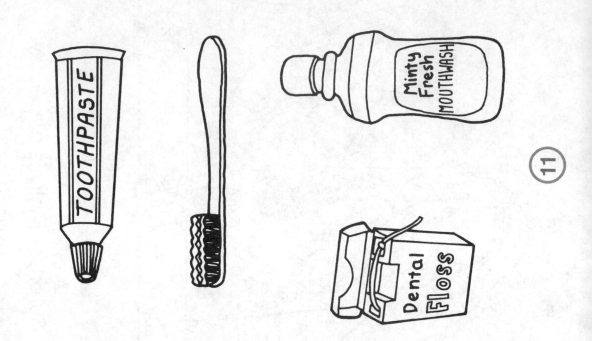

(11)

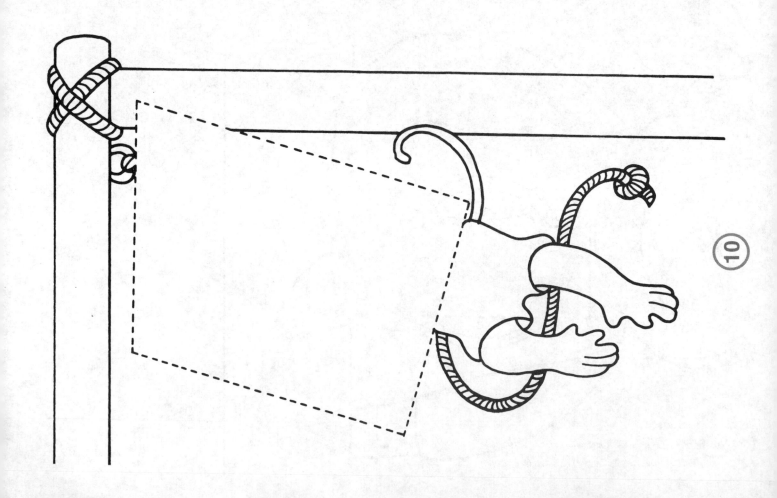

(10)

Molly's Teeth

Cut & Paste Patterns

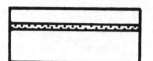

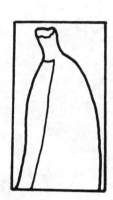

That Is When I Know!

Skill Seasons

Getting Started

Divide a sheet of chart paper into four equal sections. Label the top of each section with the name of one of the four seasons: *Winter*, *Spring*, *Summer*, or *Fall*. Then discuss one season at a time with children. Invite them to share what they know about the signs and weather related to that season. Write their responses in the corresponding section of the chart paper. After filling in all of the sections, review and compare the information about all of the seasons.

Completing the Mini-Book

Ask children to write their name on the cover, then cut out and glue the patterns onto the pages, as shown. Finally, have them complete the activity on pages 9 and 11.

Reproducible Pages
mini-book: pages 105–110
patterns: pages 111–112

That Is When I Know!

by _____

When the air is cold and snow falls all around, that is when I know it is Winter.

①

②

When a warm breeze blows and flowers start to grow, that is when I know it is Spring.

③

④

When the sun shines hot and the days are long, that is when I know it is Summer.

⑤

When the frost chills the night and the leaves fall down, that is when I know it is Fall.

⑦

⑧

Winter, Spring, Summer, and Fall.

_____ is the season I like most of all!

⑨

My Favorite Season

⑩

Trace the letters. Say the seasons.

Winter
Spring
Summer
Fall

⑪

Write a season on the line.

Trace the letters. Say the seasons.

Taking It Further

Tell children that many trees change with the seasons. For example, a leafless, bare tree is associated with Winter, a tree with budding leaves usually signals Spring, a tree full of green leaves indicates Summer, and a tree that's changing colors and shedding leaves suggests Fall. Then form small groups, give each group four sheets of paper, and instruct children to draw a tree for a different season on each sheet. Invite the groups to share their trees with the class.

When the air is cold

and snow falls all around,

that is when I know

it is Winter.

Cut & Paste Mini-Books: Science © 2011 by Nancy I. Sanders, Scholastic Teaching Resources (page 105)

That Is When I Know!

by _____

When a warm breeze blows

and flowers start to grow,

that is when I know

it is Spring.

③

Cut & Paste Mini-Books: Science © 2011 by Nancy I. Sanders, Scholastic Teaching Resources (page 106)

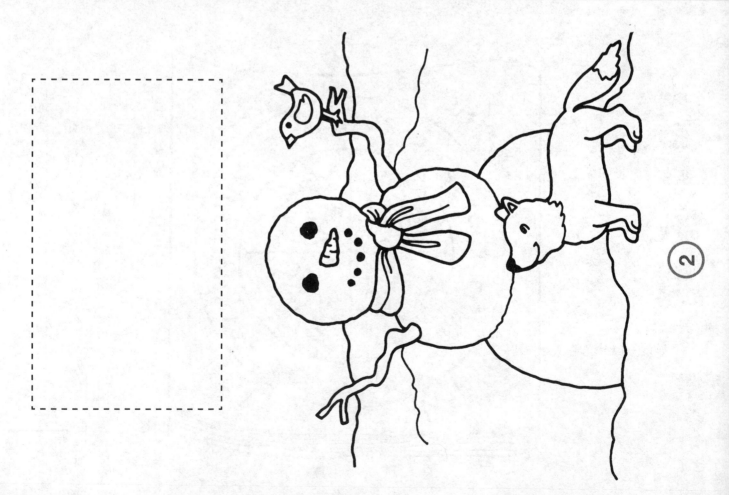

②

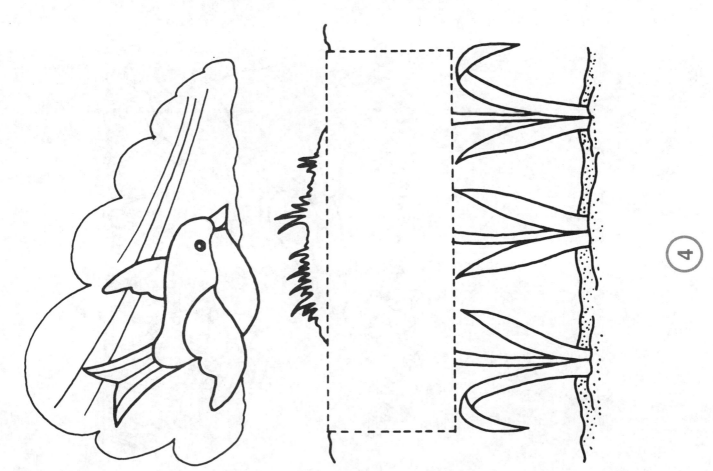

When the sun shines hot
and the days are long,
that is when I know
it is Summer.

⑤

④

When the frost chills the night
and the leaves fall down,
that is when I know
it is Fall.

Winter, Spring, Summer, and Fall.

_____ is the season

I like most of all!

⑨

⑧

Trace the letters. Say the seasons.

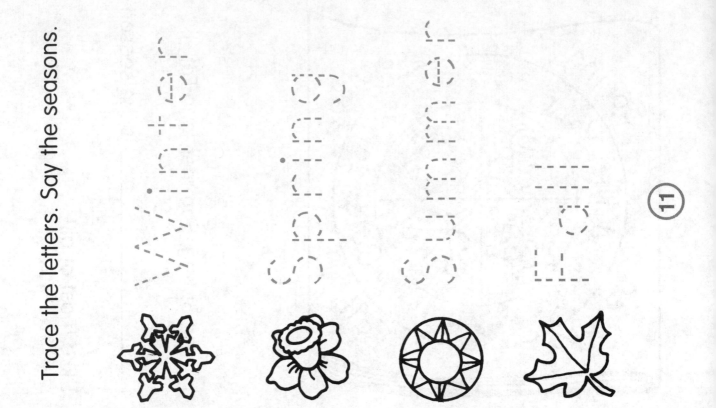

Winter

Spring

Summer

Fall

⑪

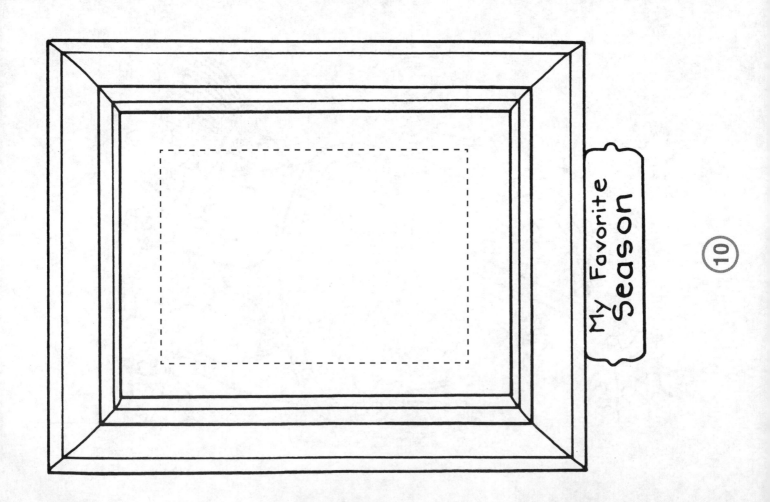

My Favorite Season

⑩

That Is When I Know!

Cut & Paste Patterns

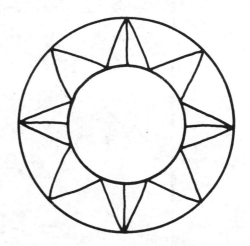

That Is When I Know!

Cut & Paste Patterns

Little Mouse's Walk

Skill Weather

Getting Started

Every day during a given week, take children on a Weather Walk. As you go along, ask children to observe the weather, sky, wind, and temperature. Back in the classroom, record children's observations on chart paper. Discuss any clues that might suggest an upcoming change in the weather, such as a light sprinkle, dark storm clouds, or cooling temperatures. Compare the charts from day to day and discuss any changes that occurred in the weather.

Completing the Mini-Book

Ask children to write their name on the cover, then cut out and glue the patterns onto the pages, as shown. Finally, have them complete the activity on the last page.

> **Reproducible Pages**
> mini-book: pages 114–119
> patterns: page 120

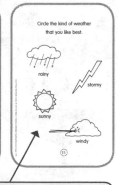

Circle the kind of weather that you like best.

Taking It Further

Stir up a storm in your classroom! First, have children rub their palms together to create the sound of wind. Then have them snap their fingers to make the sound of raindrops. Next, ask children to gently beat their thighs with open palms to mimic the sound of a heavy rain. Have them stomp their feet rapidly to make thunder. Finally, to simulate the passing of the storm, have children reverse the actions, ending with the wind slowly coming to a standstill.

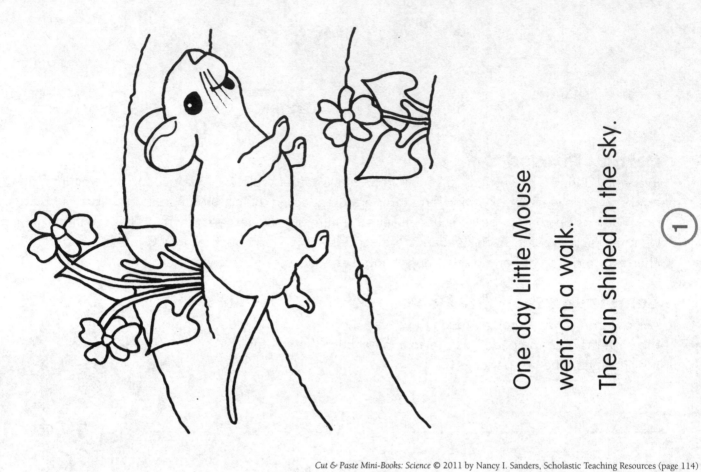

One day Little Mouse
went on a walk.
The sun shined in the sky.

Little Mouse's Walk

by _____

Then the wind started to blow.

Oh, no!

③

②

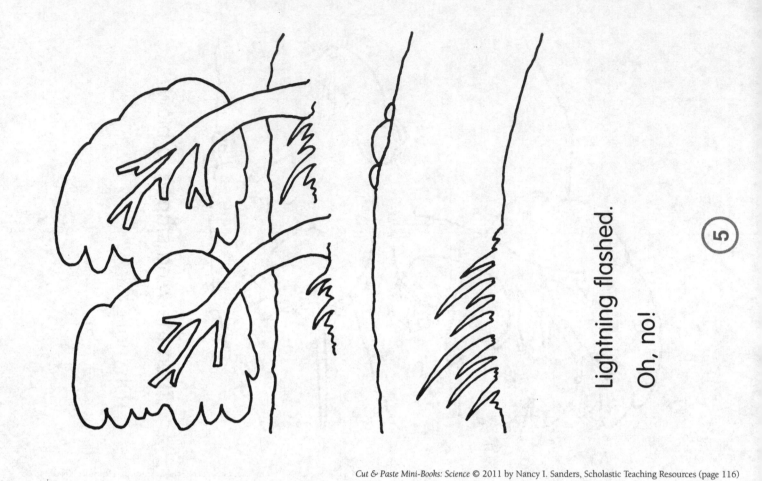

Lightning flashed.

Oh, no!

⑤

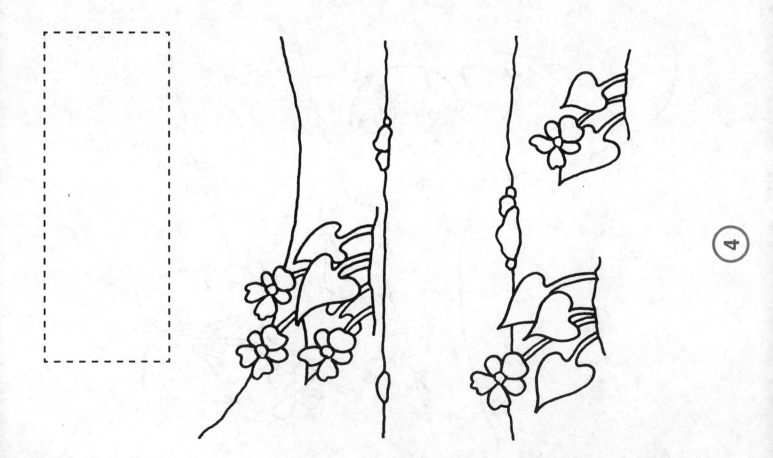

④

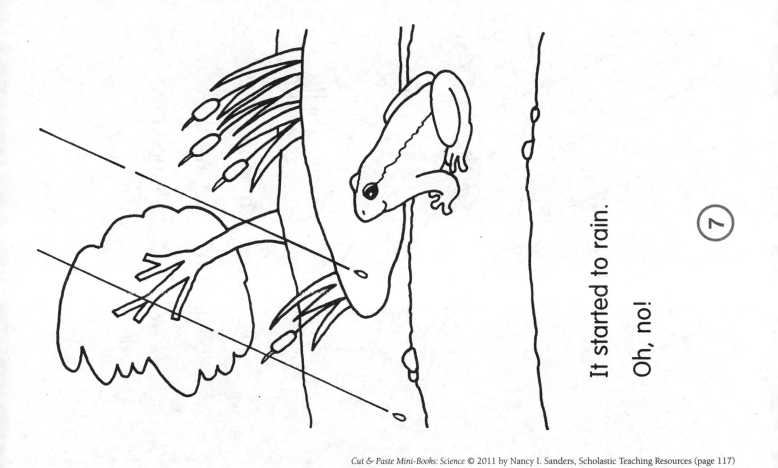

It started to rain.

Oh, no!

⑦

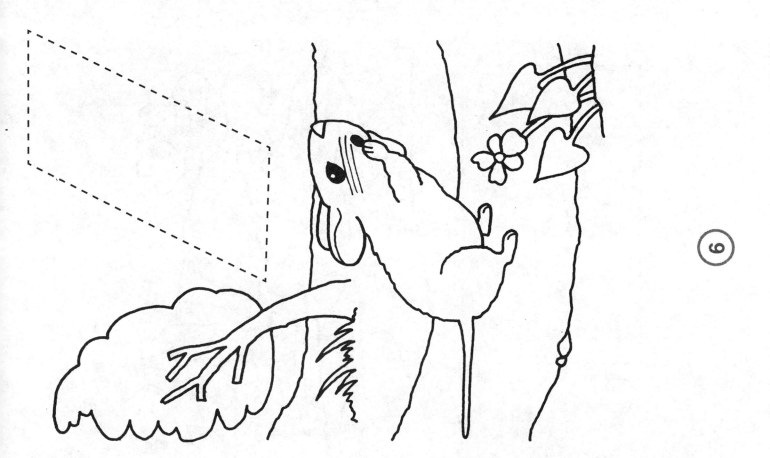

⑥

Little Mouse ran home
to his warm, cozy nest.

Now he was safe and dry.

Oh, yes!

⑨

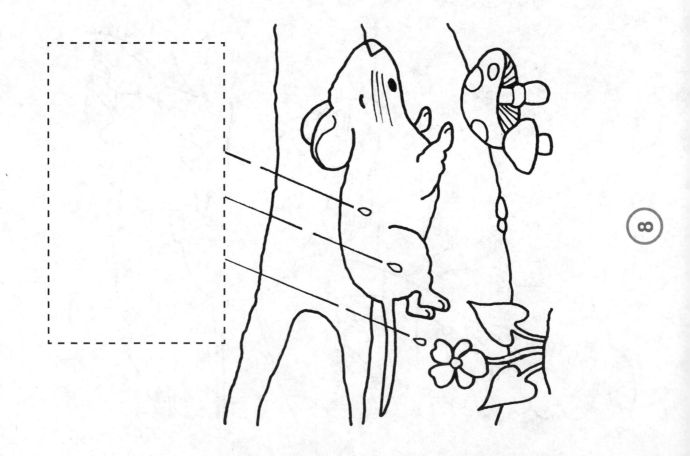

⑧

Circle the kind of weather
that you like best.

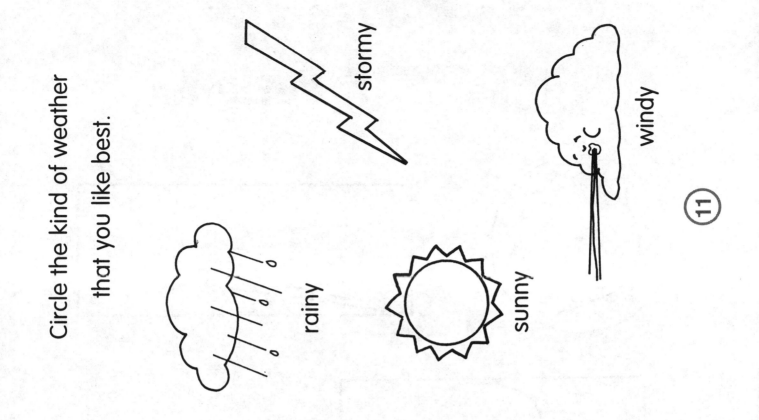

stormy

rainy

sunny

windy

(11)

Cut & Paste Mini-Books: Science © 2011 by Nancy I. Sanders, Scholastic Teaching Resources (page 119)

(10)

Little Mouse's Walk

Cut & Paste Patterns

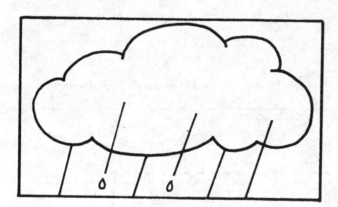

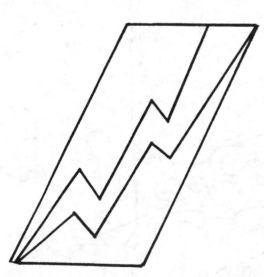

Twinkle, Twinkle

Skill Space

Getting Started

Display pictures of the Sun, stars, the Moon, a comet, and the Big Dipper constellation. Identify each object and share a little about it with children. You might tell them that a star is a burning ball of gas, the Moon circles Earth, a comet has a long tail, the Big Dipper is a group of stars that resembles a drinking cup, and the Sun is a star. Research each object, as needed, to share as much information as you wish.

Completing the Mini-Book

Ask children to write their name on the cover, then cut out and glue the patterns onto the pages, as shown. Finally, have them complete the activity on the last page.

> **Reproducible Pages**
> mini-book:
> pages 122–127
> patterns:
> page 128

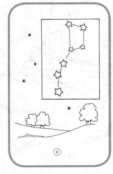

Draw two things that you can see in the night sky.

Taking It Further

Create a large, three-by-three grid. Label the columns (from left to right) "We Know…," "We Want to Know…," and "We Learned…" Label the rows (from top to bottom) "Sun," "Moon," and "Stars." Then distribute cutouts of a sun, moon, and star. Ask children to write something they know about each space object on the corresponding cutout and attach it to the left column in the row for that object. Have them write a question about each object on another cutout and attach it to the middle column. Finally, have children do research to try to answer their question. Ask them to write the answer (or a new fact) on another cutout to put in the right column.

Twinkle, twinkle in the night,

I see a star's pretty light.

(1)

Twinkle, Twinkle

by _____

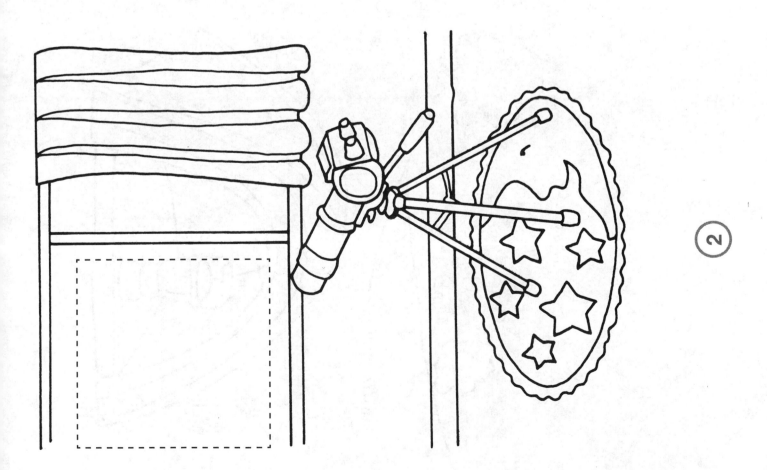

Twinkle, twinkle in the night,
I see the Moon, big and bright.

3

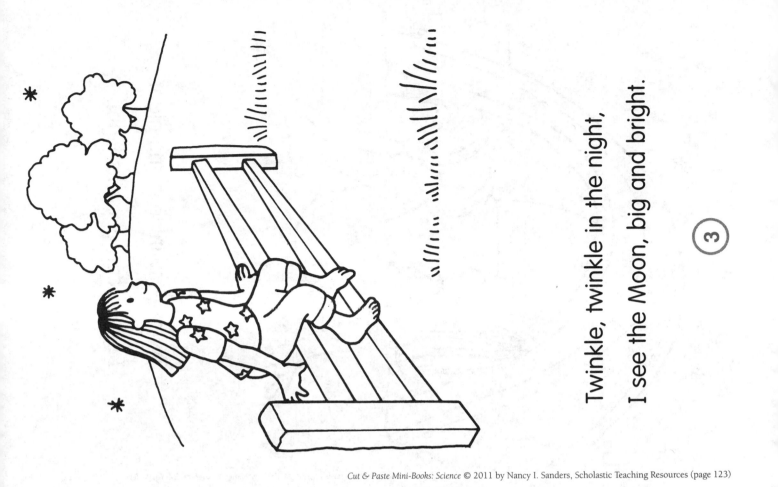

2

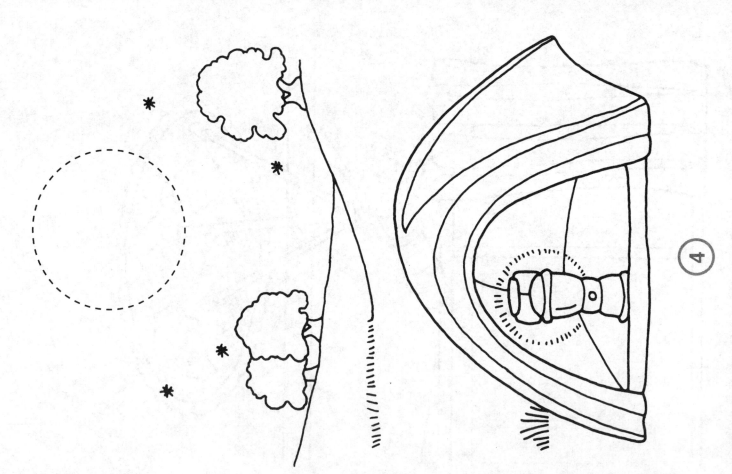

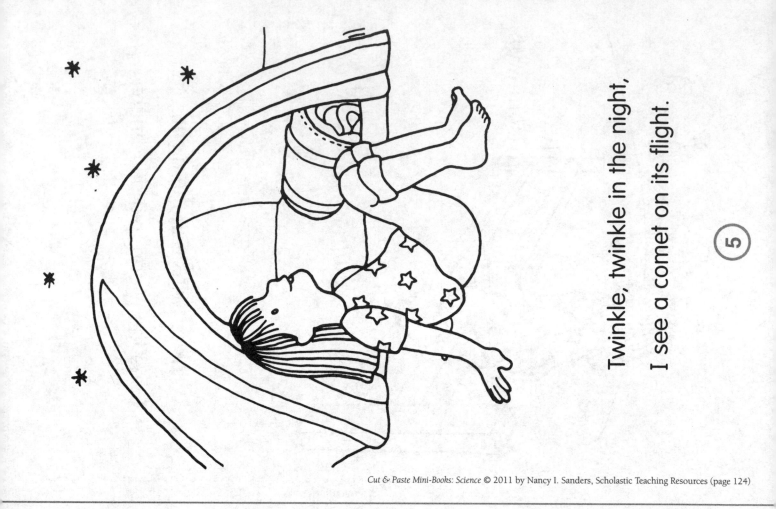

Twinkle, twinkle in the night,
I see a comet on its flight.

⑤

④

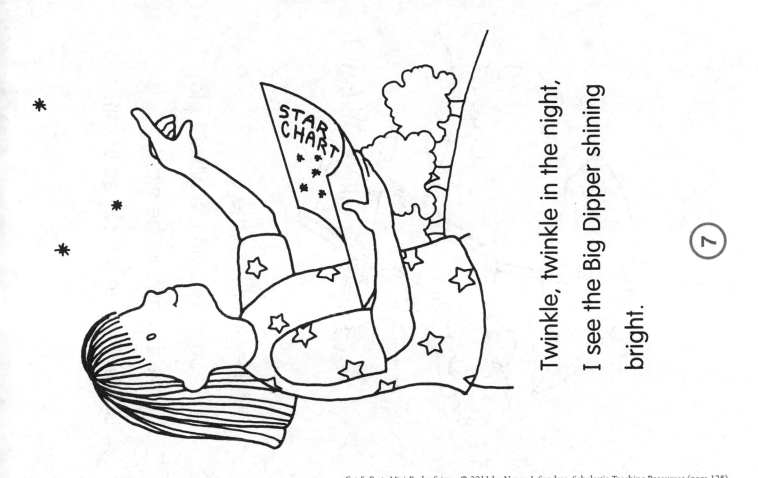

Twinkle, twinkle in the night,

I see the Big Dipper shining bright.

(7)

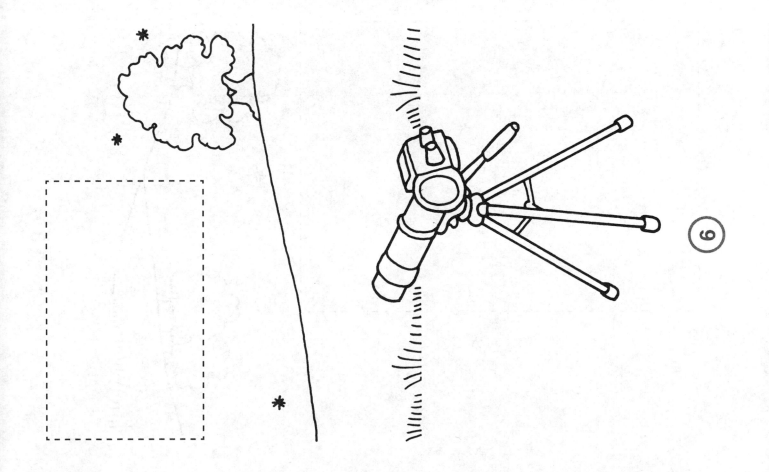

(6)

Twinkle, twinkle in the day,

The Sun shines on me while I play.

In the day and in the night,

Lights shine in the sky so bright!

Cut & Paste Mini-Books: Science © 2011 by Nancy I. Sanders, Scholastic Teaching Resources (page 126)

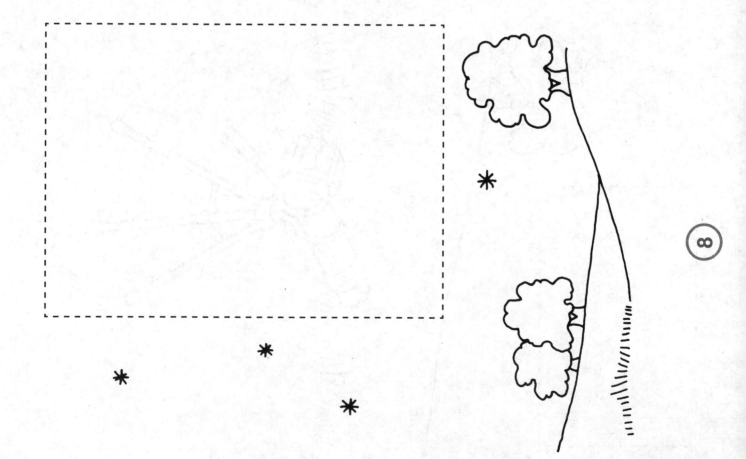

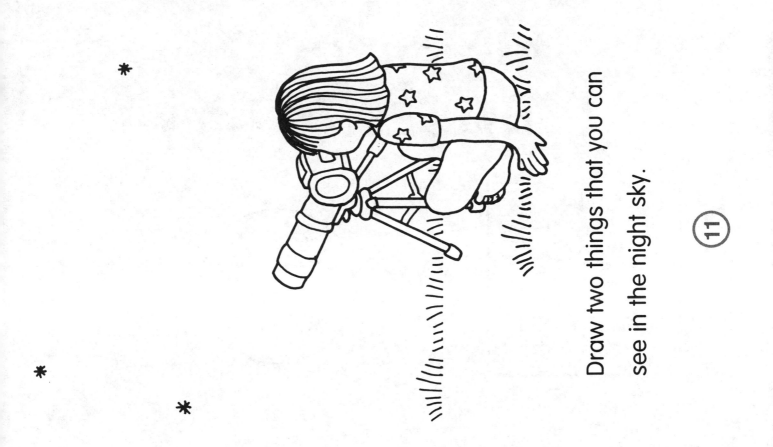

Draw two things that you can see in the night sky.

(11)

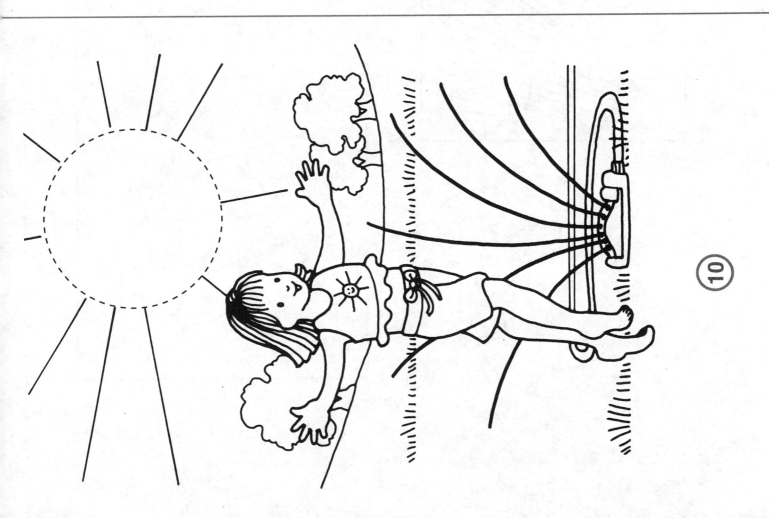

(10)

Twinkle, Twinkle

Cut & Paste Patterns

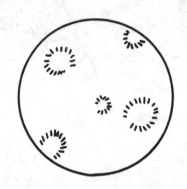

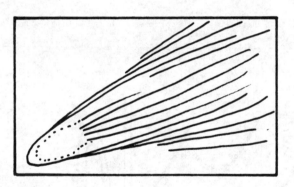

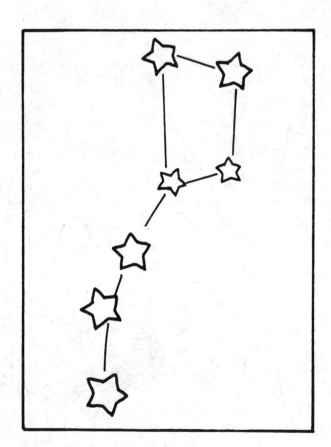

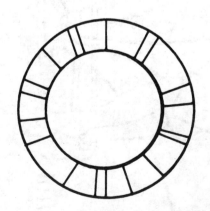